Lance Wyman: Process.
A proposal for the 1976 USA
Bicentennial identity.

Unit 41

'It's a Process. It's Not Instant.'
An interview with Lance Wyman by Adrian Shaughnessy.

The work in these pages is a record of the development of a remarkable design project. It catalogues the work of Lance Wyman – in collaboration with the architect Michael Cohalan – submitted as the entry in a competition to design a logo and graphic identity for the 1976 Bicentennial celebrations to mark the creation of the USA as an independent republic.

This work was done in Mexico in 1970. As all Wyman's admirers know, he'd gone there to design the graphics for the Games of the XIX Olympiad, otherwise known as the Mexico 68 Olympics.

After spending four years in Mexico City working on the Olympics, as well as other projects, Wyman came home to New York. It was 1971, and he returned to a design scene that was markedly different from the one he had left. For a start, he had acquired a reputation. His work for Mexico 68 was widely acclaimed, especially by clients involved in civic and public wayfinding projects, and it had been eulogised in design magazines – even the art critic of The New York Times had written a fulsome appreciation.

Wyman also returned to a country that was on the verge of officially decreeing that graphic design, and design in general, was to have a central role in Federal policy. One year after Wyman's return to New York, Richard M Nixon, the 37th President of the USA, initiated the Federal Design Improvement Program, a far-ranging initiative run by the National Endowment of the Arts.

Much of the success of the Federal Design Improvement Program can be attributed to Nancy Hanks. As the visionary head of the NEA, she established the Program with the intention of raising the importance of design amongst Federal agencies, and for many prominent designers such as Saul Bass, Ivan Chermayeff, Richard Saul Wurman, Lou Dorfsman and Eliot Noyes, the Program was enthusiastically welcomed.

Wyman was to work on numerous projects that came from this enterprise, some of them amongst the most celebrated of his career: National Zoo (1975), Washington Mall (1975), Minnesota Zoo (1979). But before any of these large-scale civic projects, and before he had even returned to the USA, Wyman took part in a competition to design the graphics for the Bicentennial celebrations which were to take place in 1976. As can be seen in the pages that follow, Wyman approached the task with his customary mix of graphic rigour and visual ingenuity.

As he explains, what we see here is a record of the process that he went through to arrive at a refined and workable solution. It's rare for designers to reveal so much of their inner workings, and even rarer for it to be documented with this degree of thoroughness. But Lance Wyman is no ordinary designer.

Adrian Shaughnessy: I'd like to begin by asking you to say what the work in this book is?

Lance Wyman: *What we have is a reproduction of a book I made as a record of the work done for a competition to design a logo and graphics for the Bicentennial celebrations planned to celebrate the USA's 200th birthday in 1976. There are proposals for the symbol and how it could be translated into architecture. There is also a proposal for a typeface, for merchandise, and for various environmental applications. I really just wanted to document the work for my own use. At that time, I was having things bound in leather because in Mexico it was quite inexpensive. I worked very hard on this project, and actually won the competition. But then, as I'll explain later, it all fell apart.*

AS: This was a competition run by the American Revolution Bicentennial Commission to find a symbol and graphics programme for the national celebrations in 1976. How did you come to be involved? Did the Commission know you from your Mexico Olympics work?

LW: *I don't know for sure that they were aware of it. I was also known for the work I'd done with George Nelson before going to Mexico in 1966. I had worked in the Nelson office, and I worked with George personally on a project for the United States Information Agency (USIA) for an exhibition in the USSR of American industrial design. We used an adaption of the US flag for the main symbol.*

AS: There's a letter from you to the Commission, and it's written from Mexico. I like your address!

LW: *Oh yes. Nebraska 35, that was our address in Mexico City. Every time I came through customs in Texas they'd mention it because Nebraska was the University of Texas's big football rival. But yes, I'd been in Mexico since 1966, and I was on the point of returning to the USA when the competition came up.*

AS: Was there a brief from the Commission?

LW: *I don't remember a brief. There must have been one, I suppose. I remember the Commission was quite formal. I had to have a letter from my banker stating my financial stability! You can see the letter at the back of this book. Ultimately this formality worked against me. Because although I won the competition, I didn't end up doing the work because I didn't have a US office with staff.*

AS: Did you work alone?

LW: *I worked with my wife Neila's brother, Michael Cohalan. He's an architect, and back then had a practice in Washington DC. I flew Michael down, and we put in an intensive week of effort. It's a good example of combining graphics and architecture. It was taking a visual idea and pushing it into physical spaces.*

AS: Did you present the work to the Bicentennial Commission in person?

LW: *I went to Washington with all the work on slides – you can see a list of the images I presented at the back of this* book. The presentation was in an old building, and in order to get the slides onto the screen, I had to project them through the bottom of a chandelier. As a result, all my images had a decorative top to them. Maybe that helped [laughs].

AS: Can you say something about the design thinking that went into the symbol?

LW: I'd used a lot of parallel lines for the Olympics, which was inspired by the pre-Hispanic cultures of Mexico. As I've already mentioned, I had worked with the US flag before. Traditionally, no-one used the flag for commercial purposes, or altered it in any way. But I think the Brits broke that down in the 1960s when the Union Jack was used in fashion and music. I must say, I enjoyed the freedom to work with the flag. I had the idea of the flag in motion, the motion of cloth.

AS: There is also the use of the numerals 7 and 6. They are used quite subtly, was that intentional?

LW: Actually, my first thought was to just use the numerals. But then I got the idea of combining them with the flag, and yes, I was concerned that the numerals were too subtle.

AS: But the Bicentennial Commission must have liked them because you won the competition.

LW: Well, yes, I did. But I don't have any letters saying that I'd won. I remember a lot of telephone calls back and forth. And I remember it getting tricky because they were not sure I could handle the job. They let me keep going, and I did some other studies, but by this time they were talking to other people, and I knew it was all over. In the end, the symbol and graphics were designed by Bruce Blackburn at Chermayeff & Geismar Associates.

AS: What do you think now when you look back at the Bicentennial work?

LW: I still the like the idea of the flag made from the 7 and 6, and I still like the aesthetic. We had a very short space of time, and we worked our butts off during the day. In the evening we'd drink tequila, and often we'd come back and start working again. So I look back and see hard work and fun.

AS: What would you like a young designer, raised in the digital age, to take away from the work here?

LW: The hardest thing to teach is having a concept, a new idea that can become a good solution. With the computer there is a tendency to start with the final refined solution. But this misses out on an important step – first establishing a unique concept. With every job, I'd pin everything to the wall in search of that magic idea. It's really easy to sabotage yourself by trashing something – by thinking – too obvious, corny, crude, etc…. I've found that if I keep my ideas in front of me, even if I've sabotaged some, I have the visual evidence of what had happened and I can rethink. So yes, there is a role for this book to show process, to show how a concept is the first step, and how it is refined over time. It's a process. It's not instant.

A proposal for the 1976 USA Bicentennial identity.

The work shown here is Lance Wyman's response to a competition brief set by the American Revolution Bicentennial Commission to design graphics for the Bicentennial celebrations.

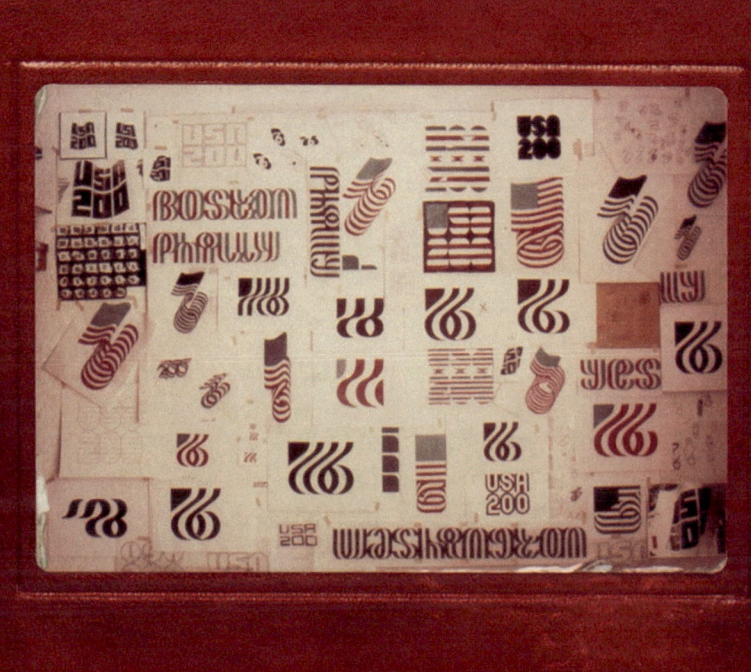

The following work sketches were drawn by Michael Cohalan, Architect AIA, and myself. They represent our initial thinking in the development of a coordinated design system for the Bicentennial celebration of our country.

Lance Hyman

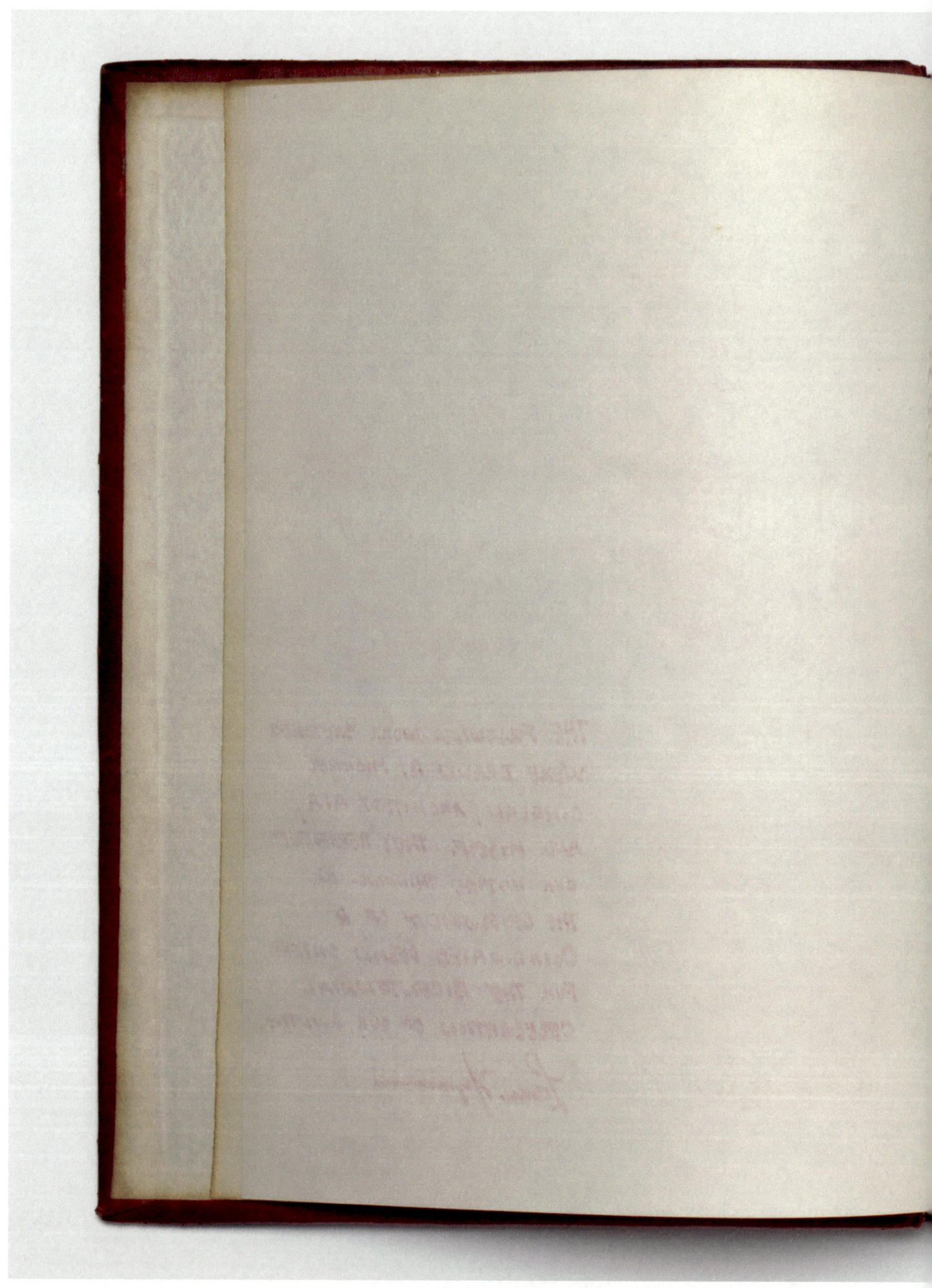

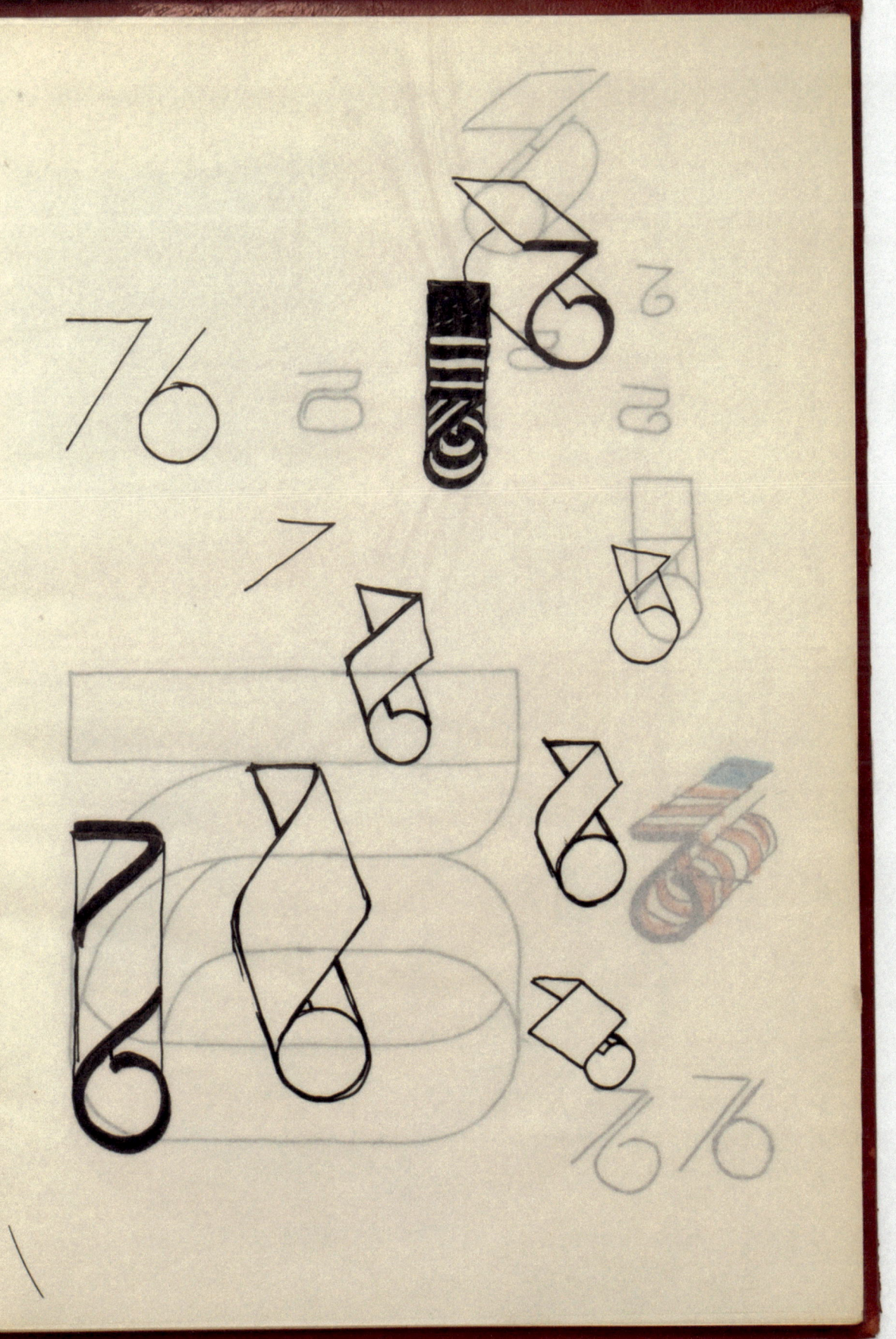

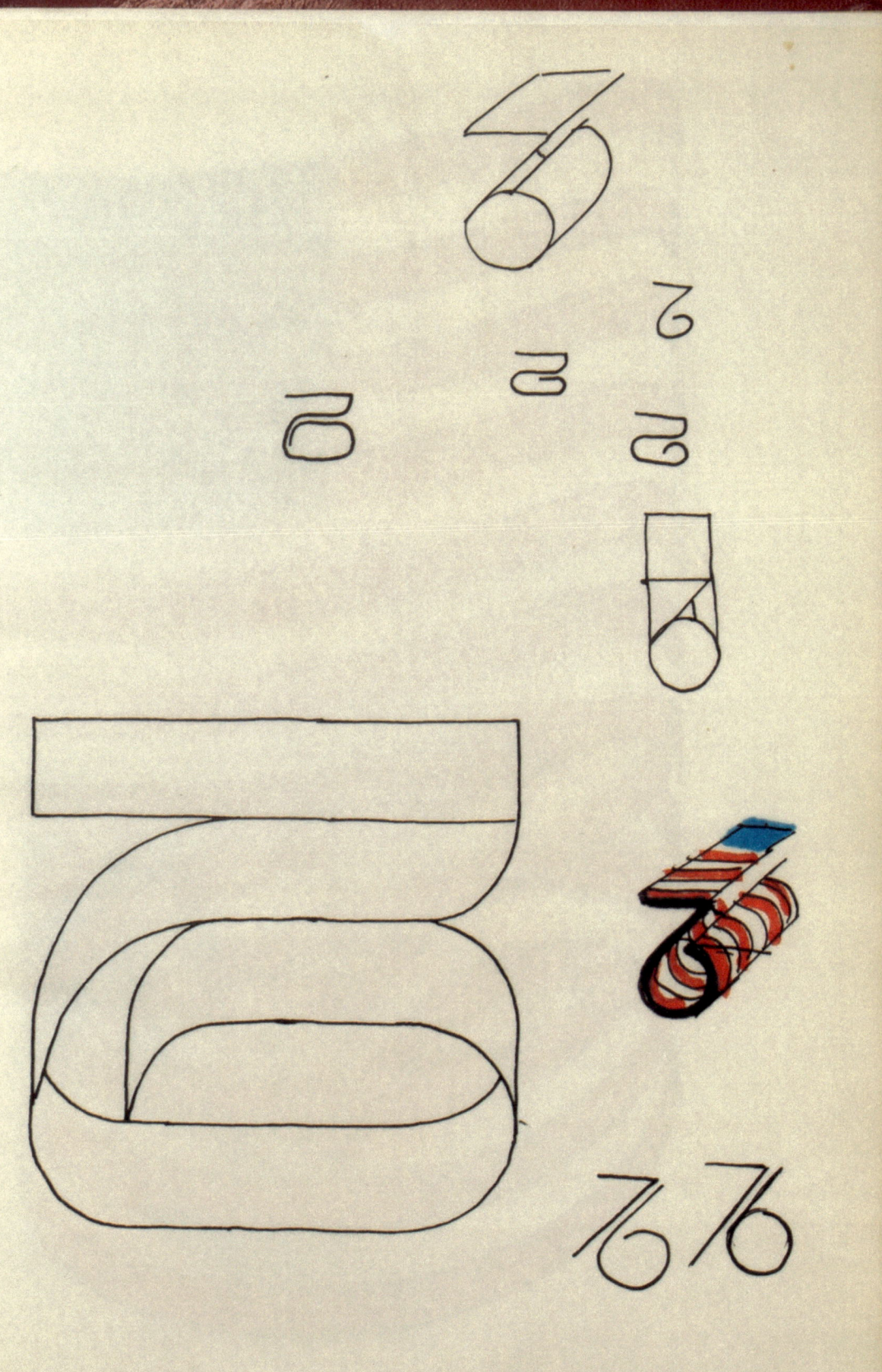

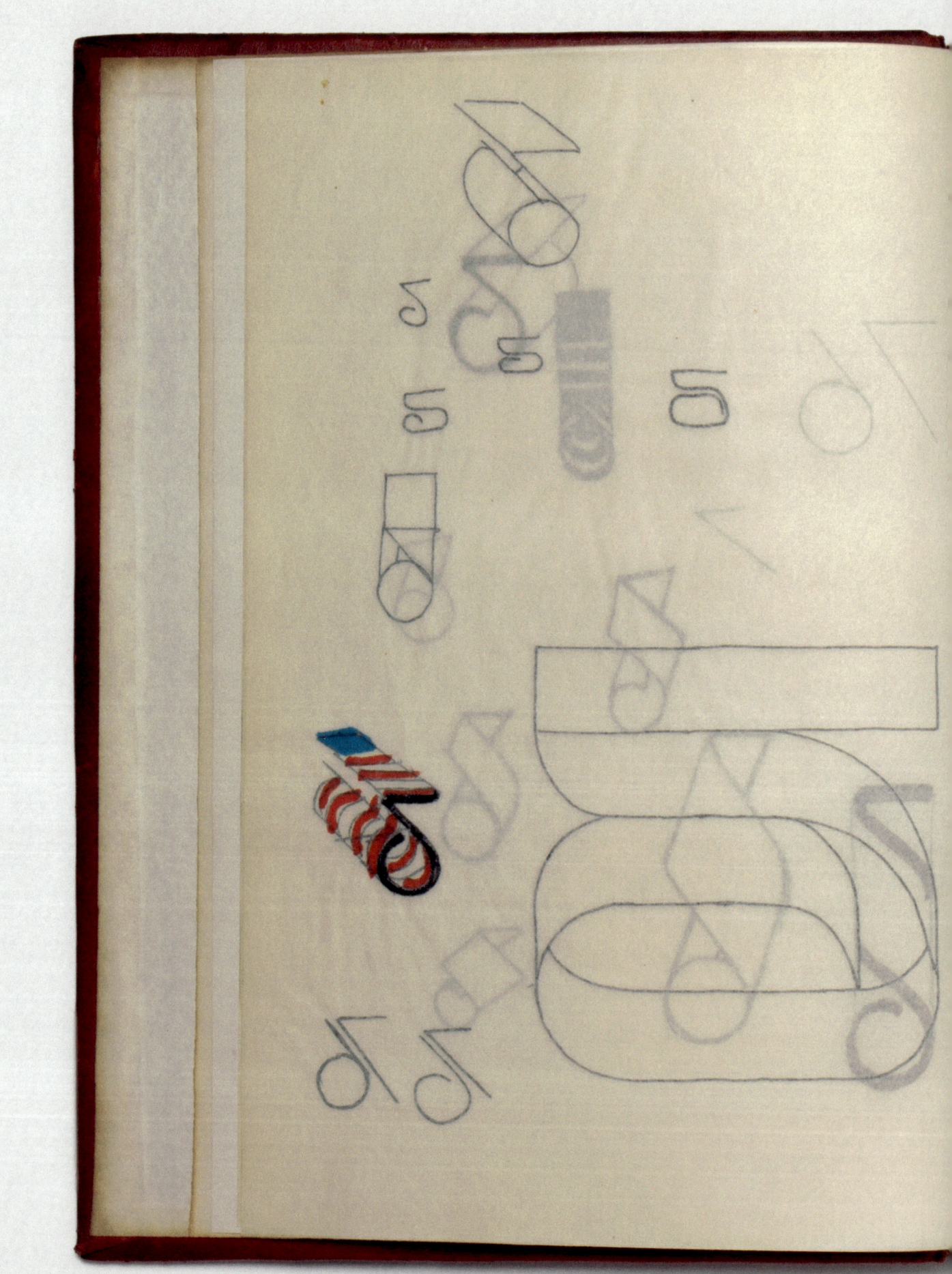

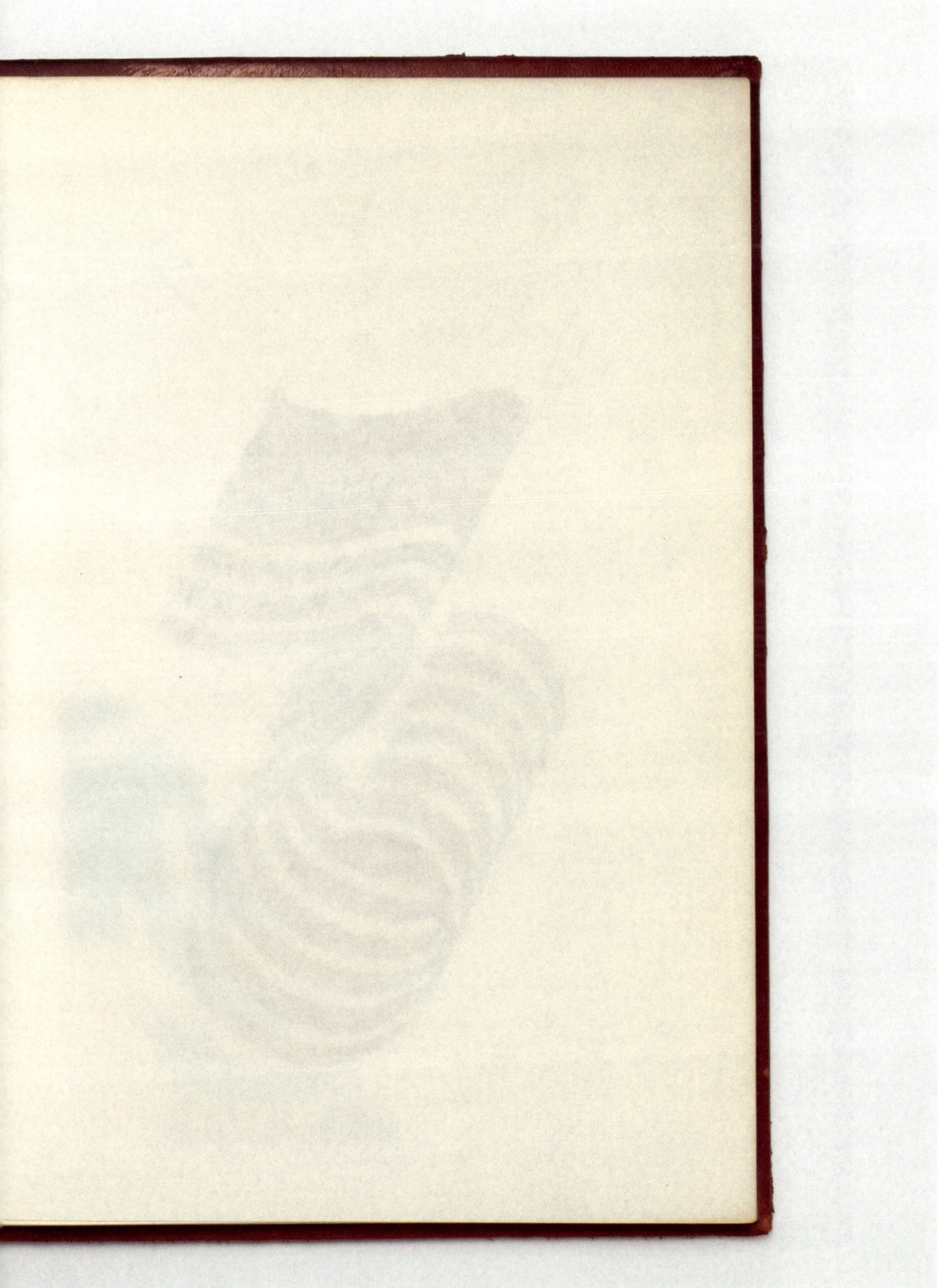

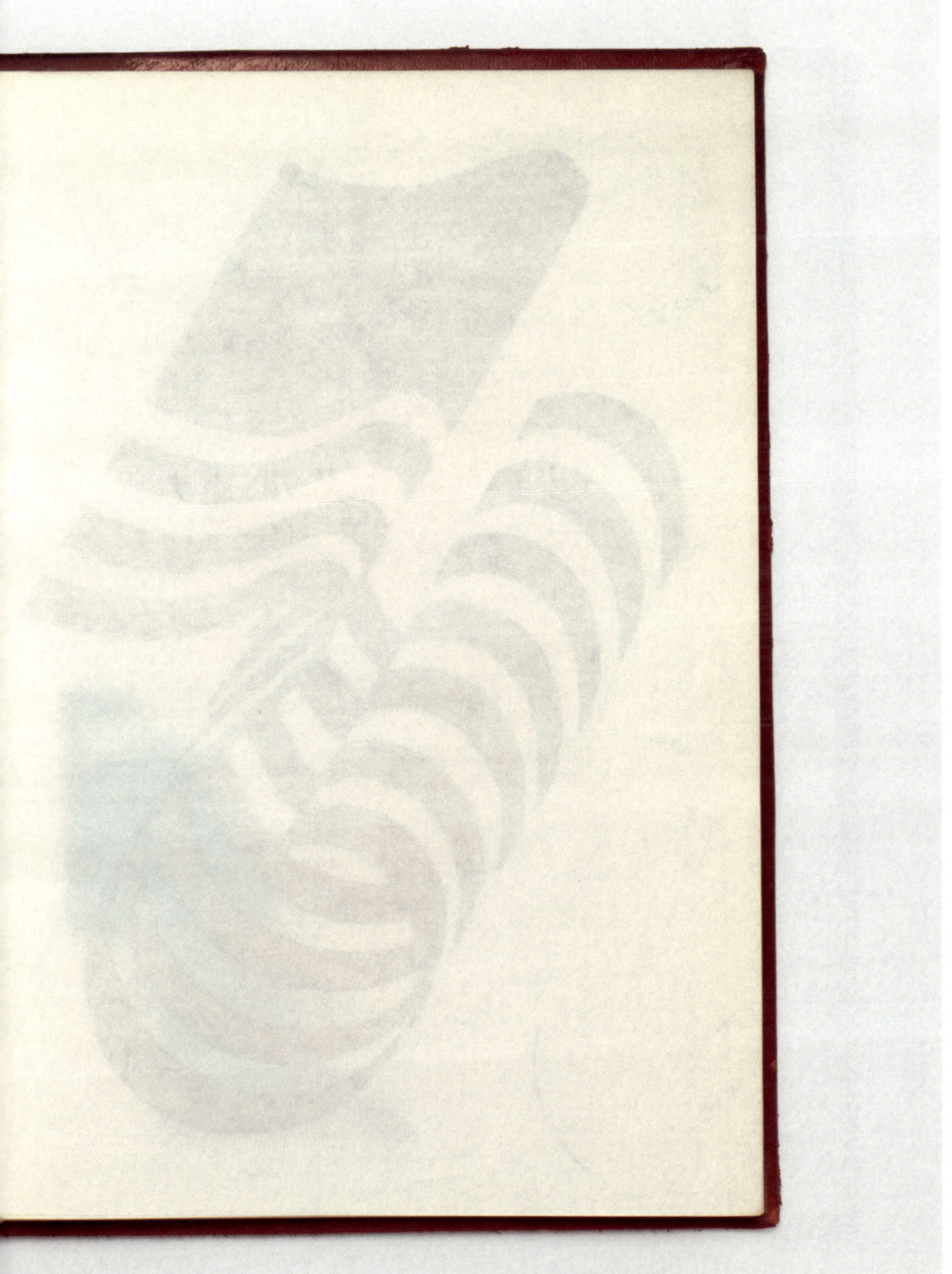

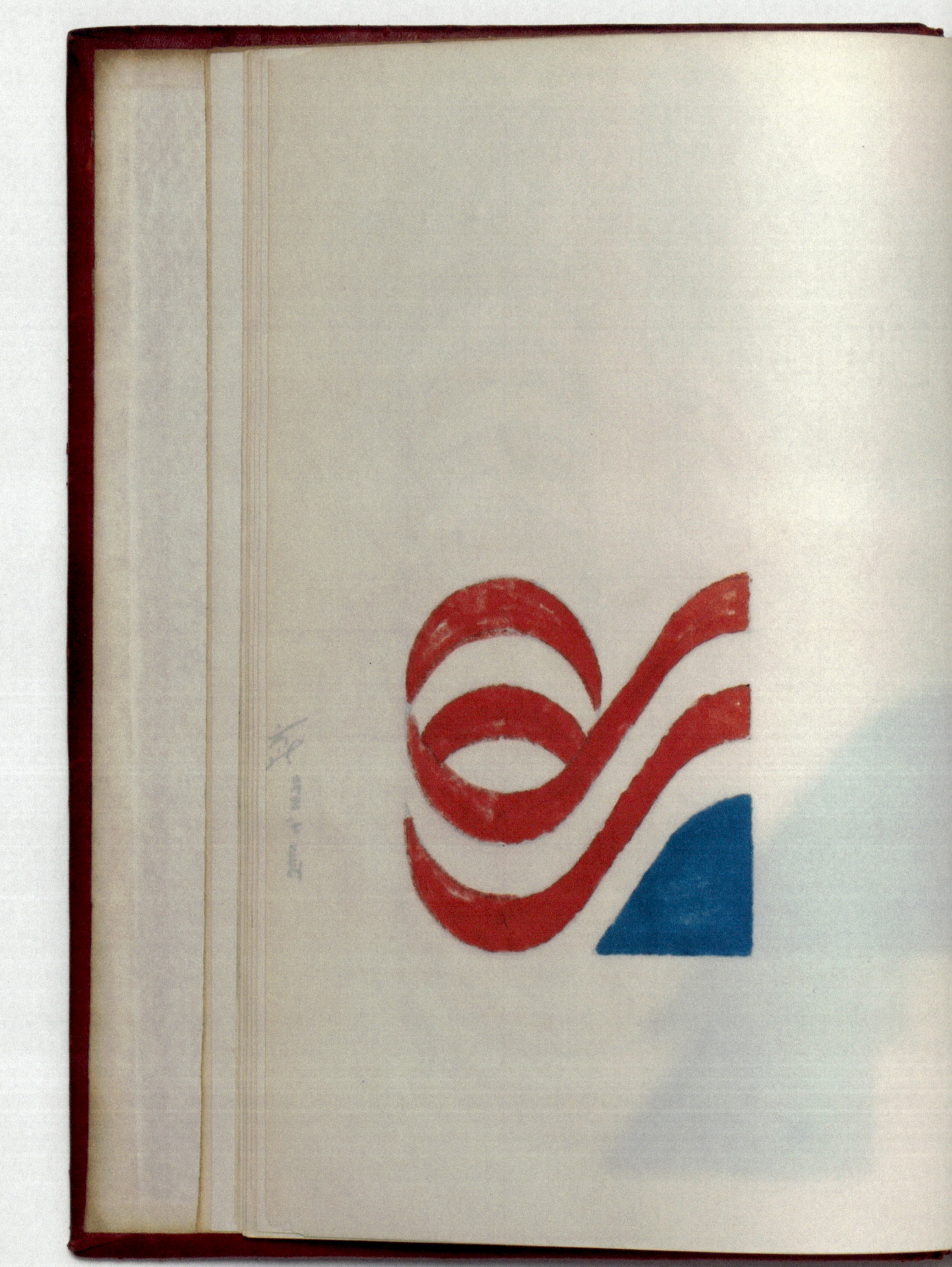

BORDERS

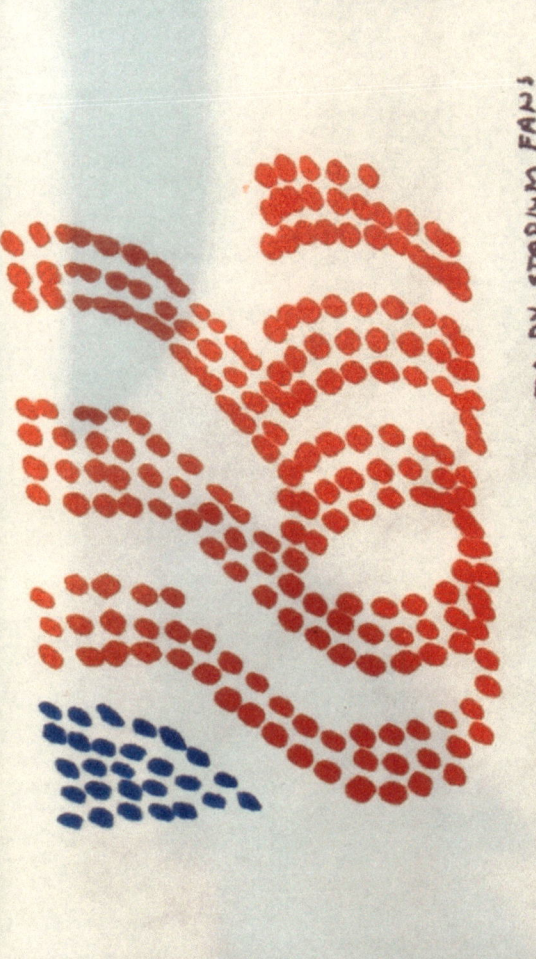

MADE OF 12 LIGHTS — CANDS HELD BY STADIUM FANS
SMALL ELEMENTS SPOT LIGHTS — FLOWERS —

Banner

3-D Banners
(TOTEM POLES)

BABRELIEF

BUTTONS

REPETITIONS

DESIGN MANUAL

TALK WITH MIKE

INFORMATION CENTERS FOR PEOPLE VISITING PLACES

1. MULTI-LINGUAL
2. ACCESS TO COMPUTERIZED PROGRAM
3. ACCESS TO RESERVATION MAKING

MAP SYSTEM (PICTORIAL) — MAKE THE CITY A MAP — COLOR CODE STREET FURNITURE LINES

ENTRANCES TO THE CITIES

LIGHTED ACCESS GATEWAY OVER THE OCEAN PROJECT ON CLOUDS

B16

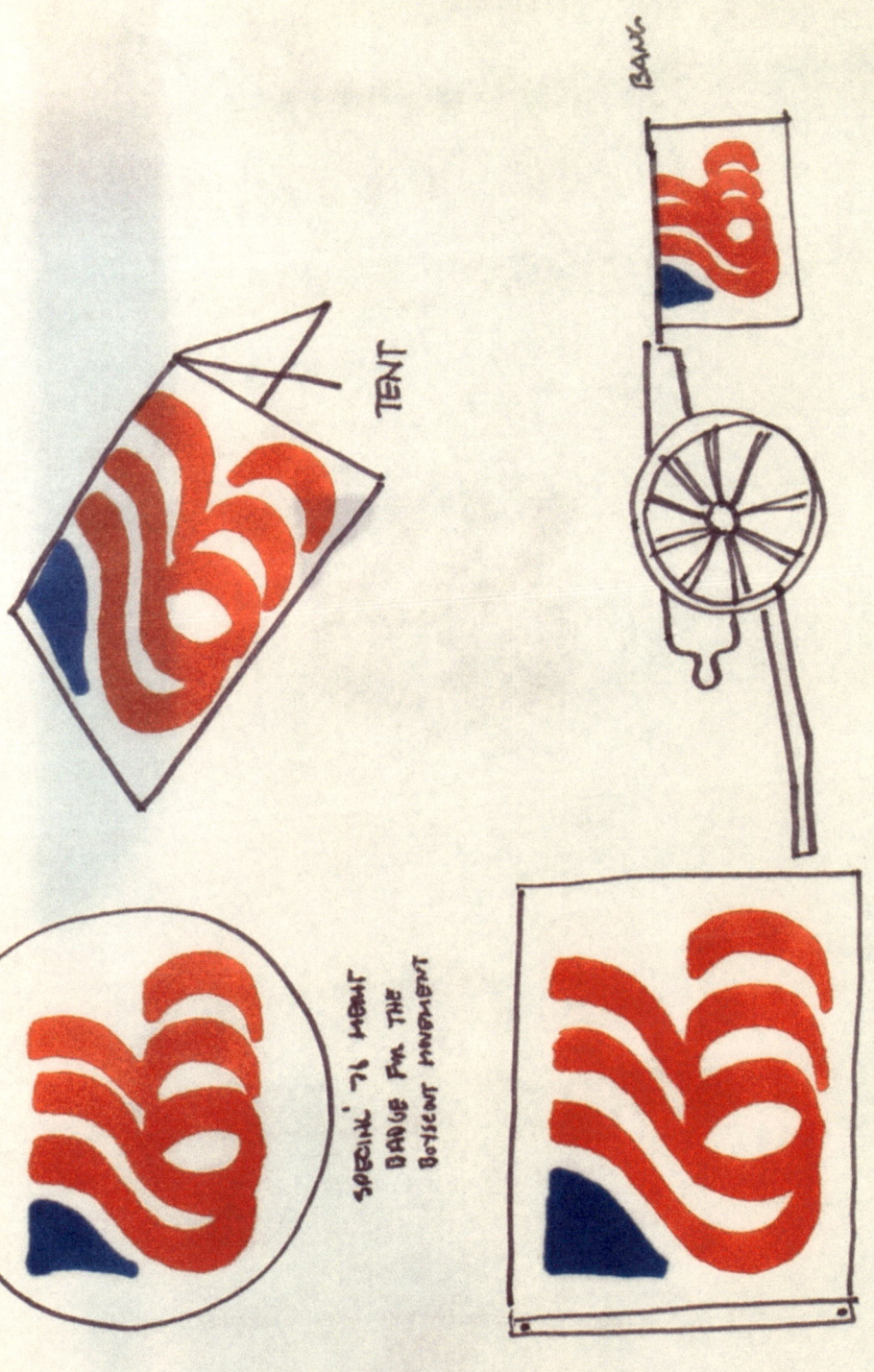

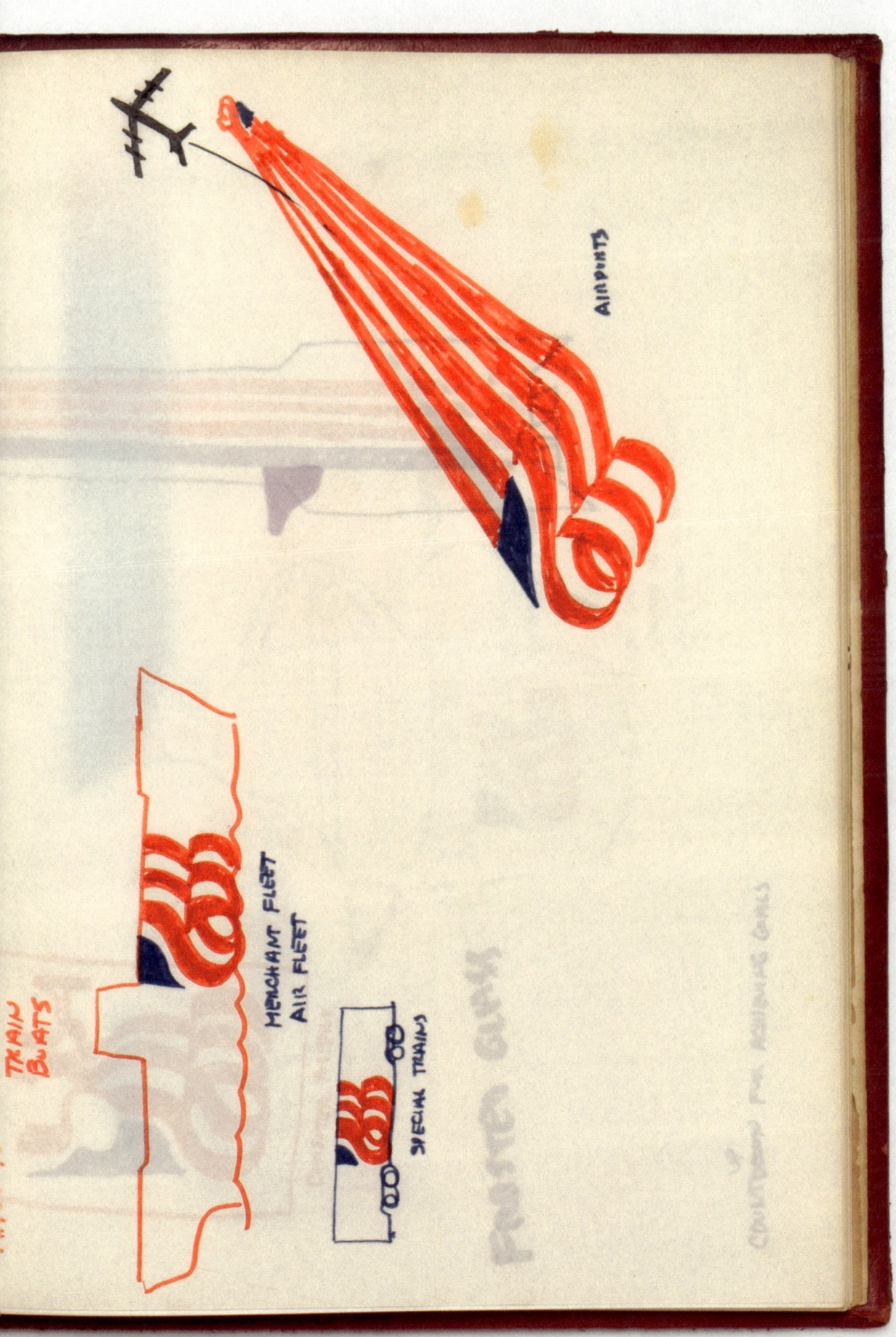

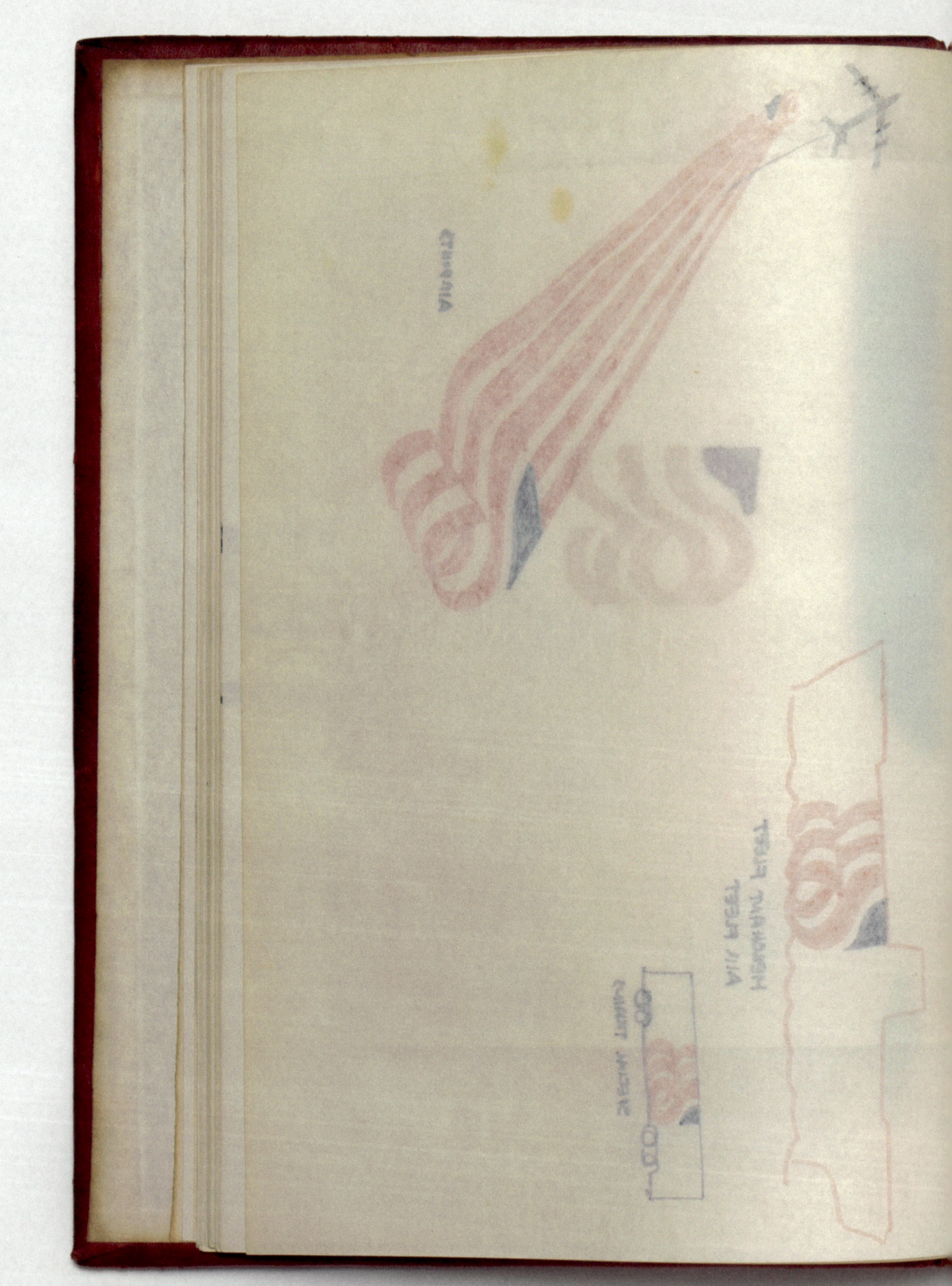

FROSTED GLASS

UP
COUNTDOWN FOR ACHIEVING GOALS

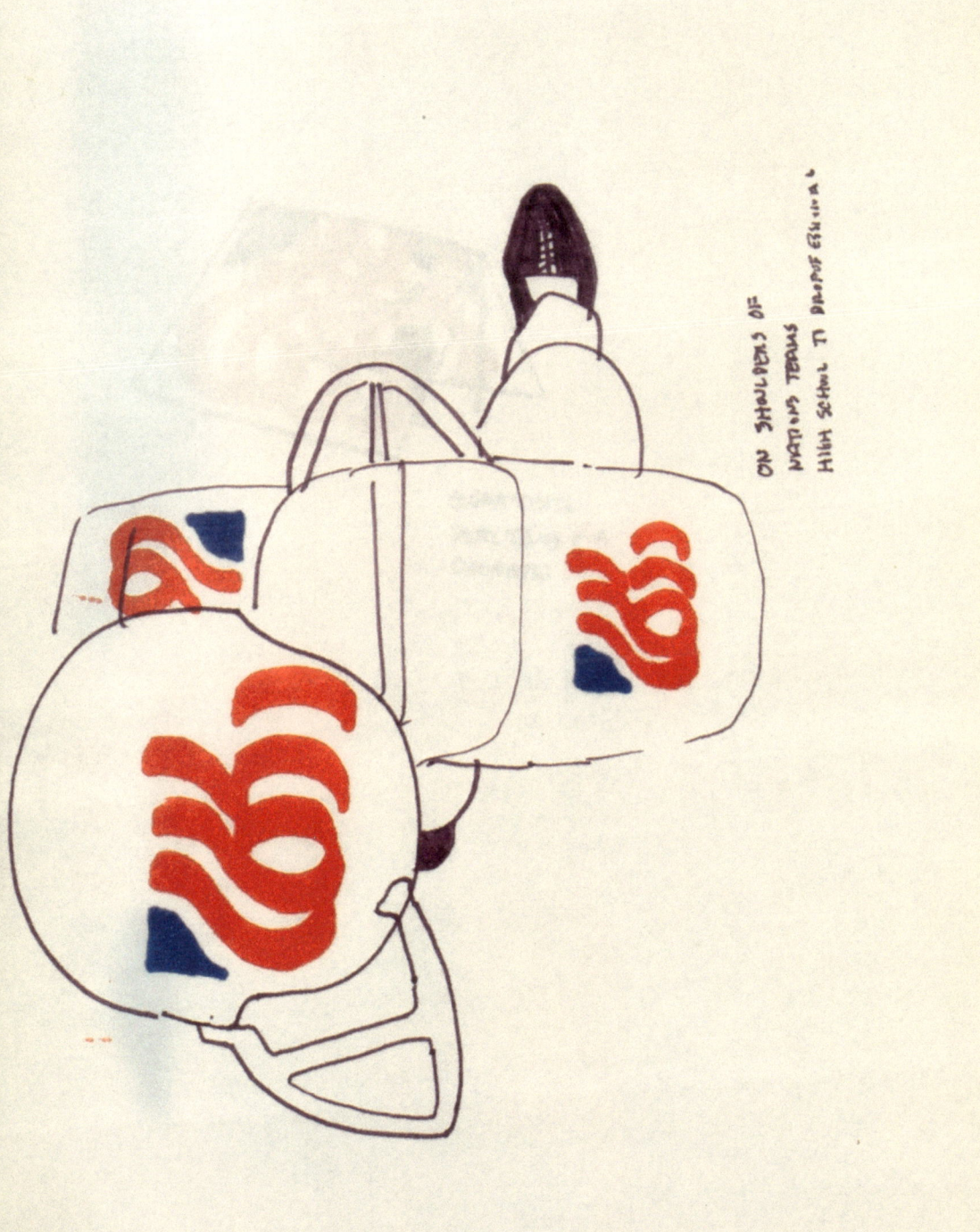

ON SHOULDERS OF NATIONS TEAMS HIGH SCHOOL TT DROP OF ETHIOPIA

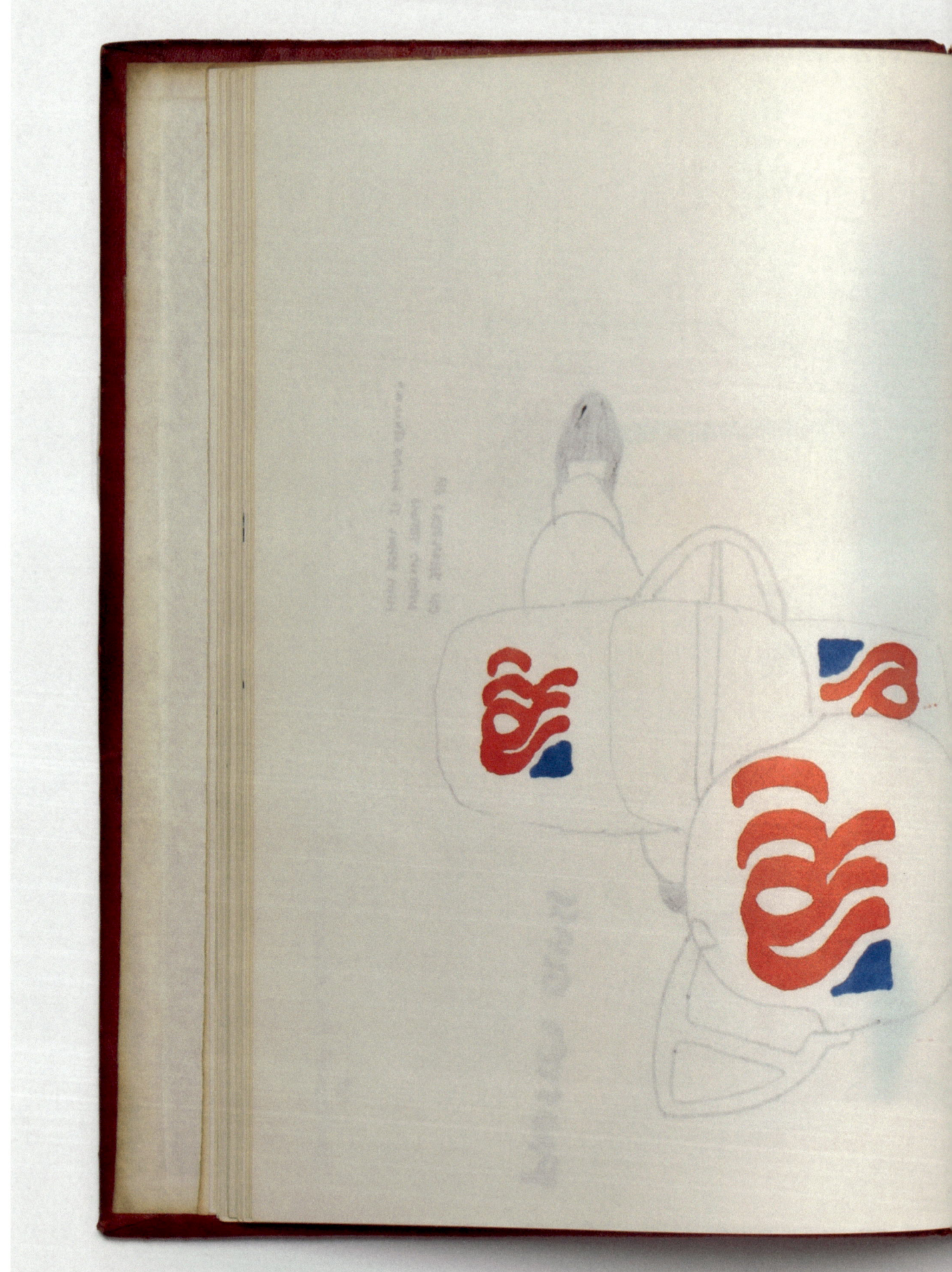

CLEAR VINYL
PLAY TENTS FOR
CHILDREN

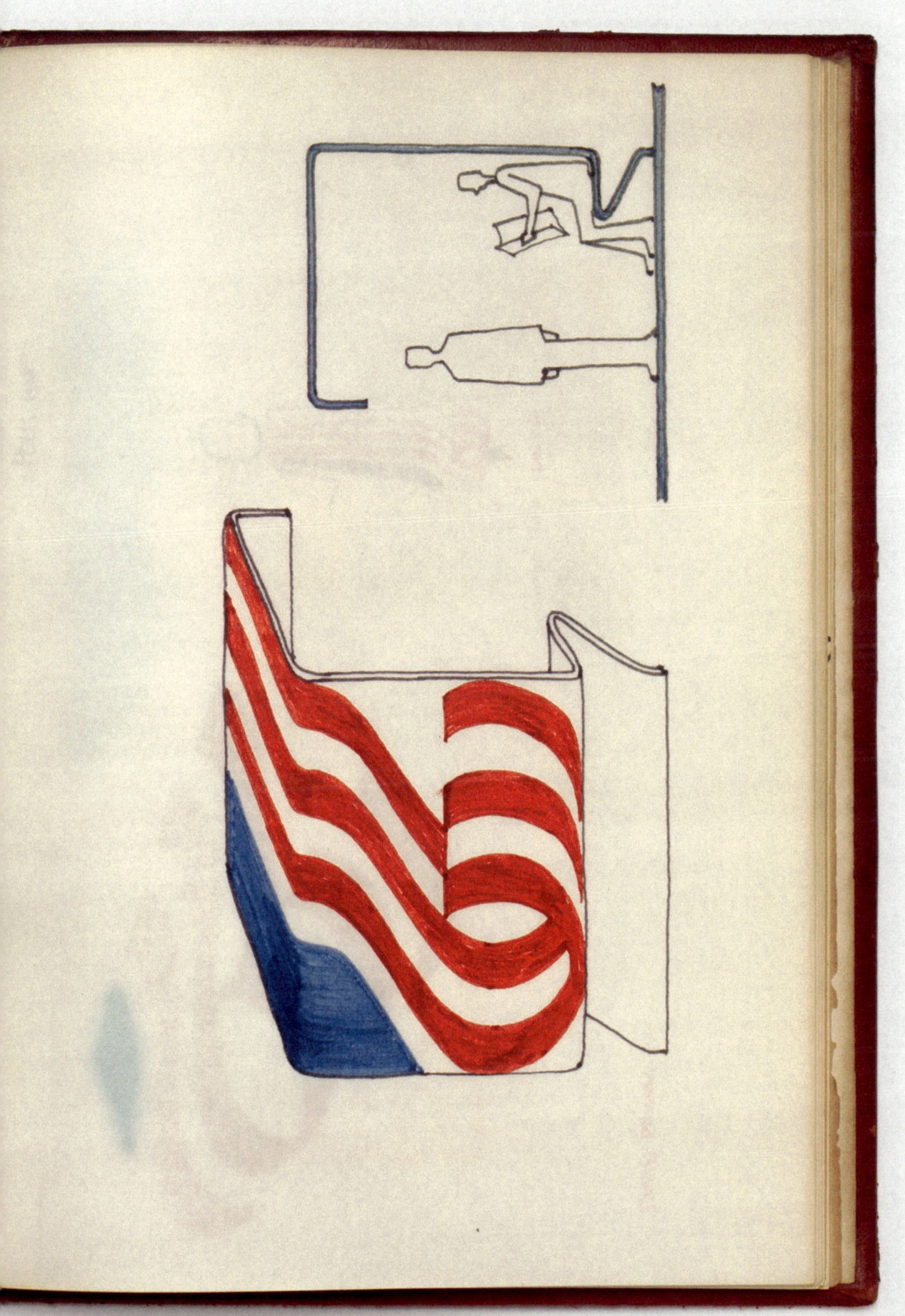

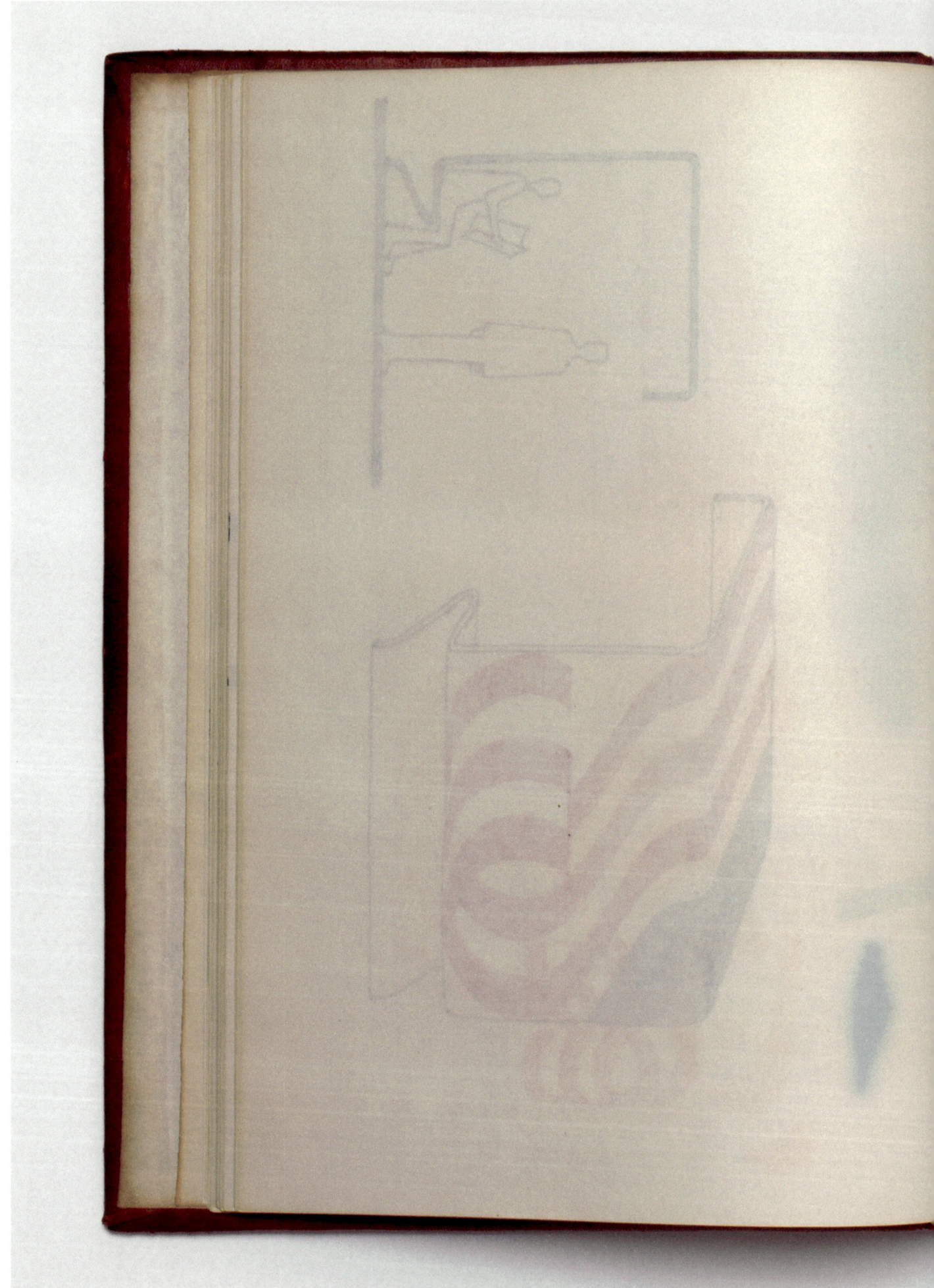

POLIS MAP

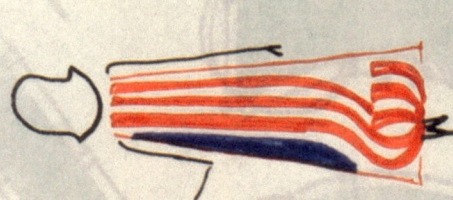
DRESSES

PLAZAS

TOURIST PROGRAMME —

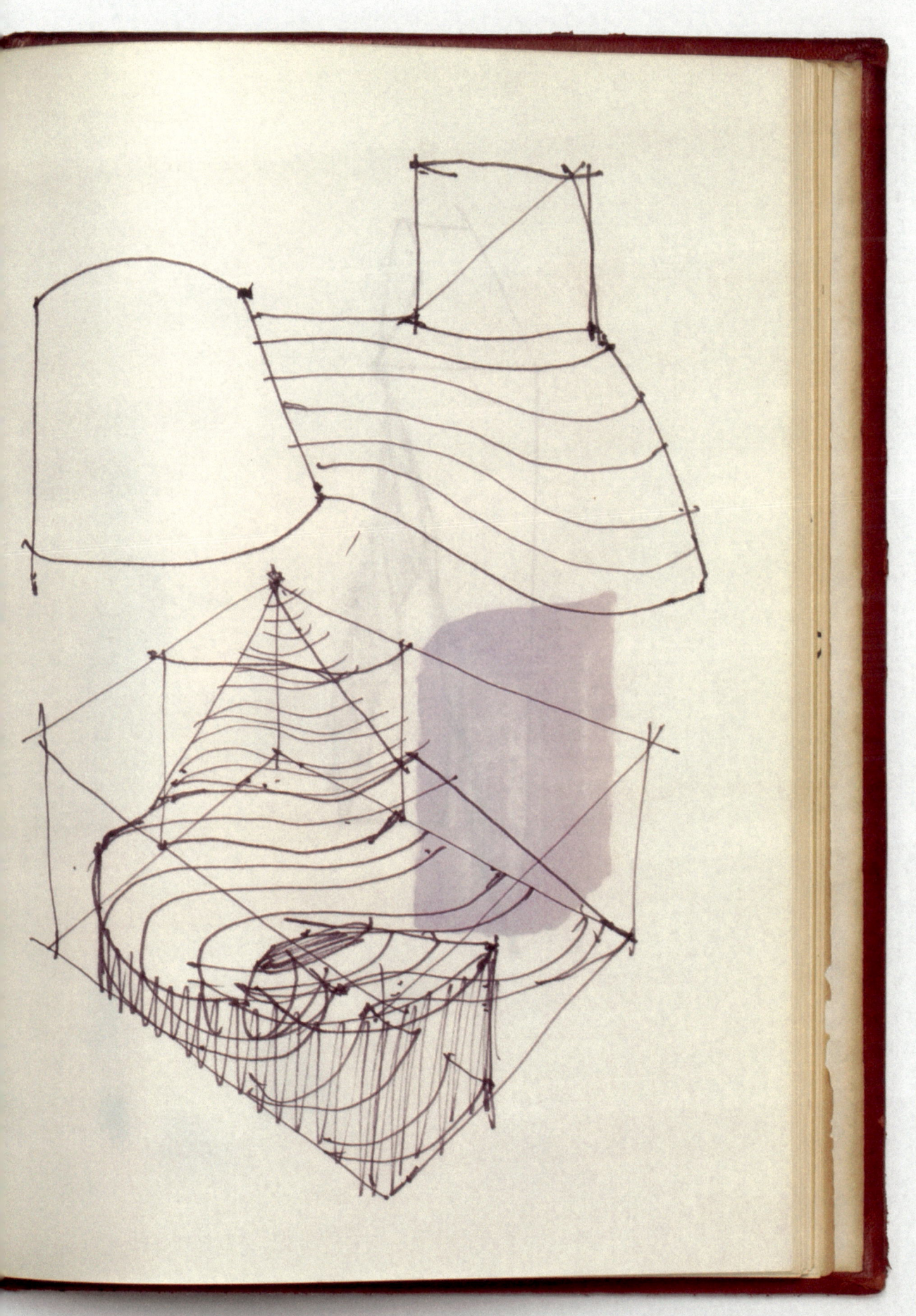

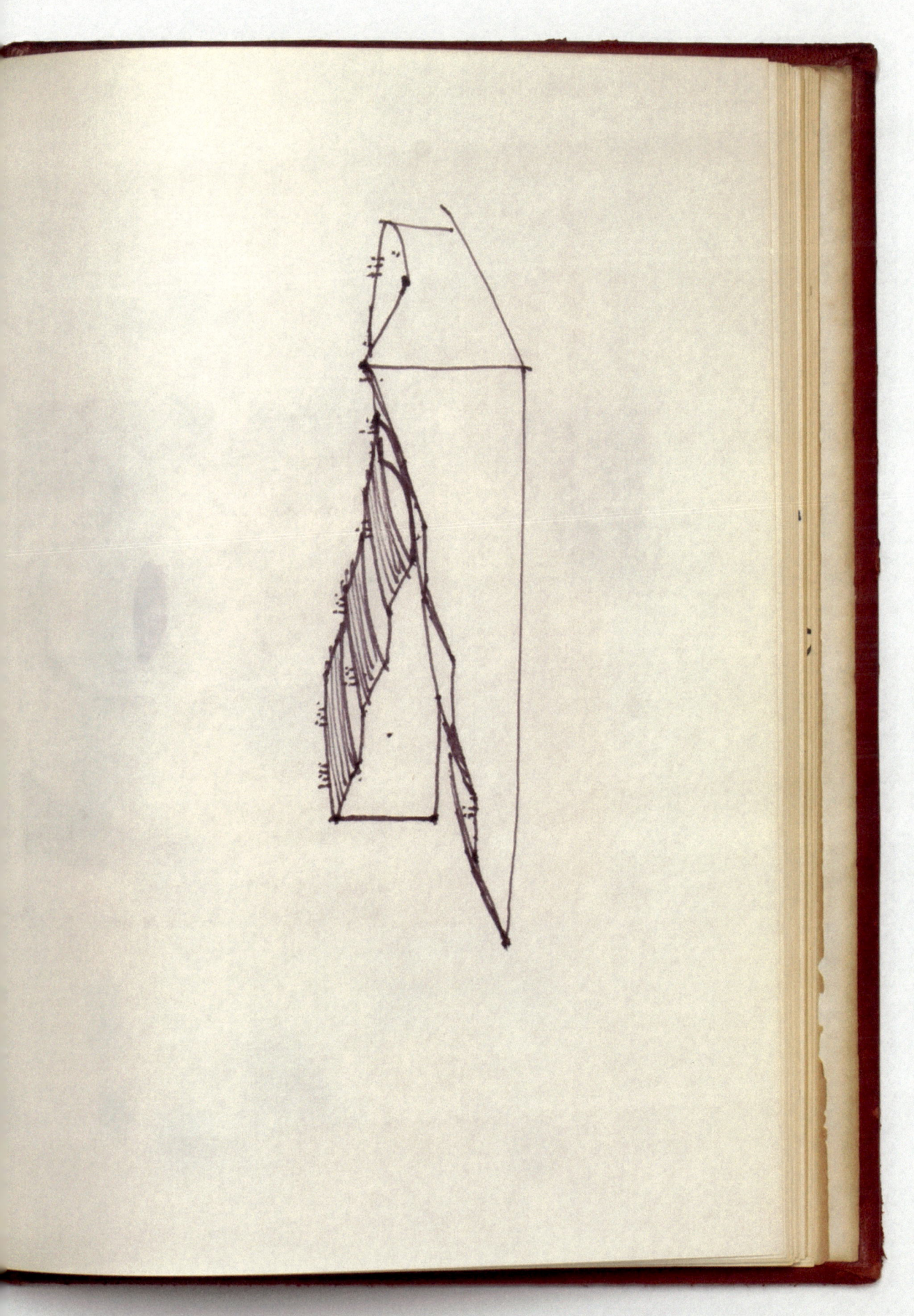

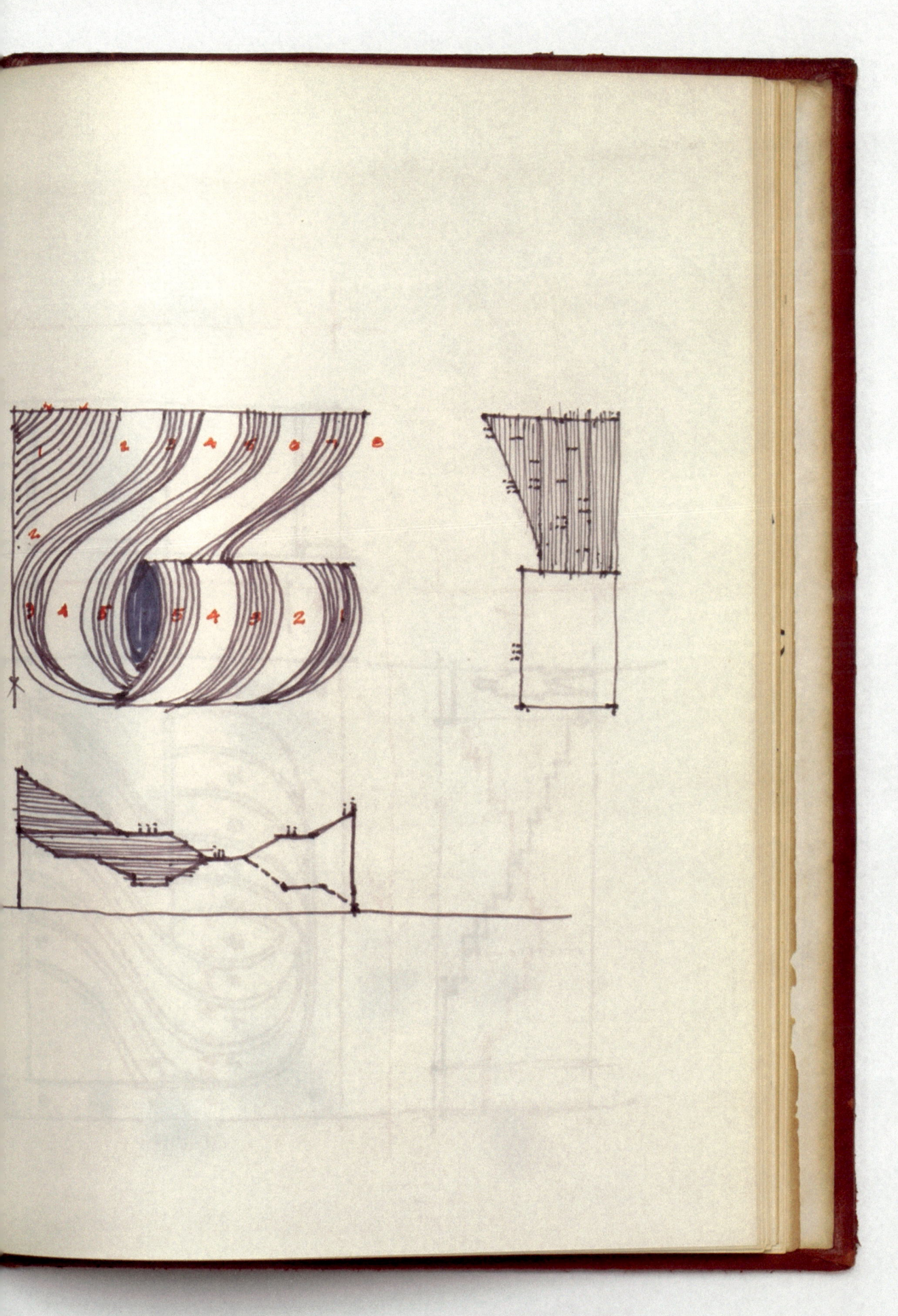

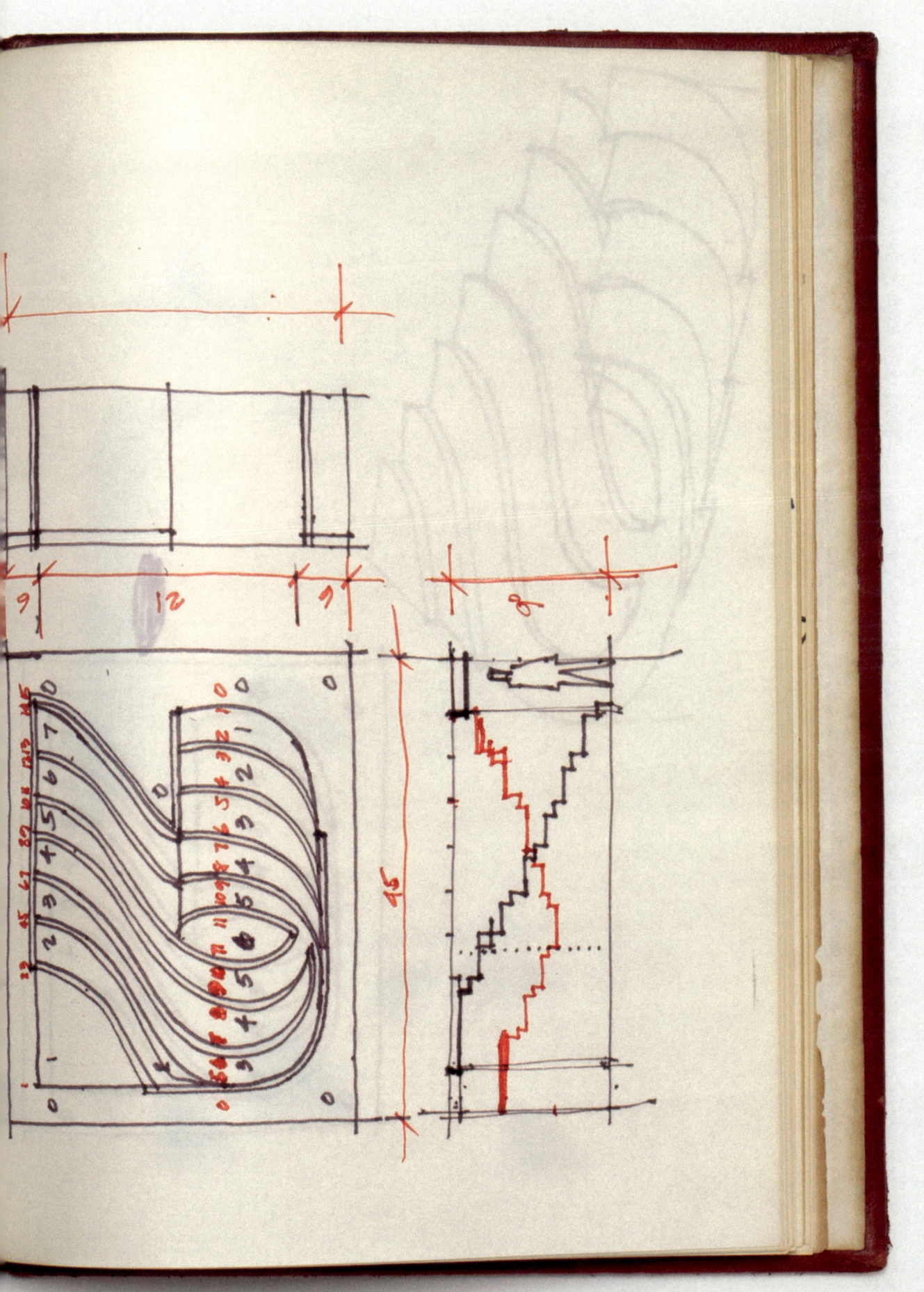

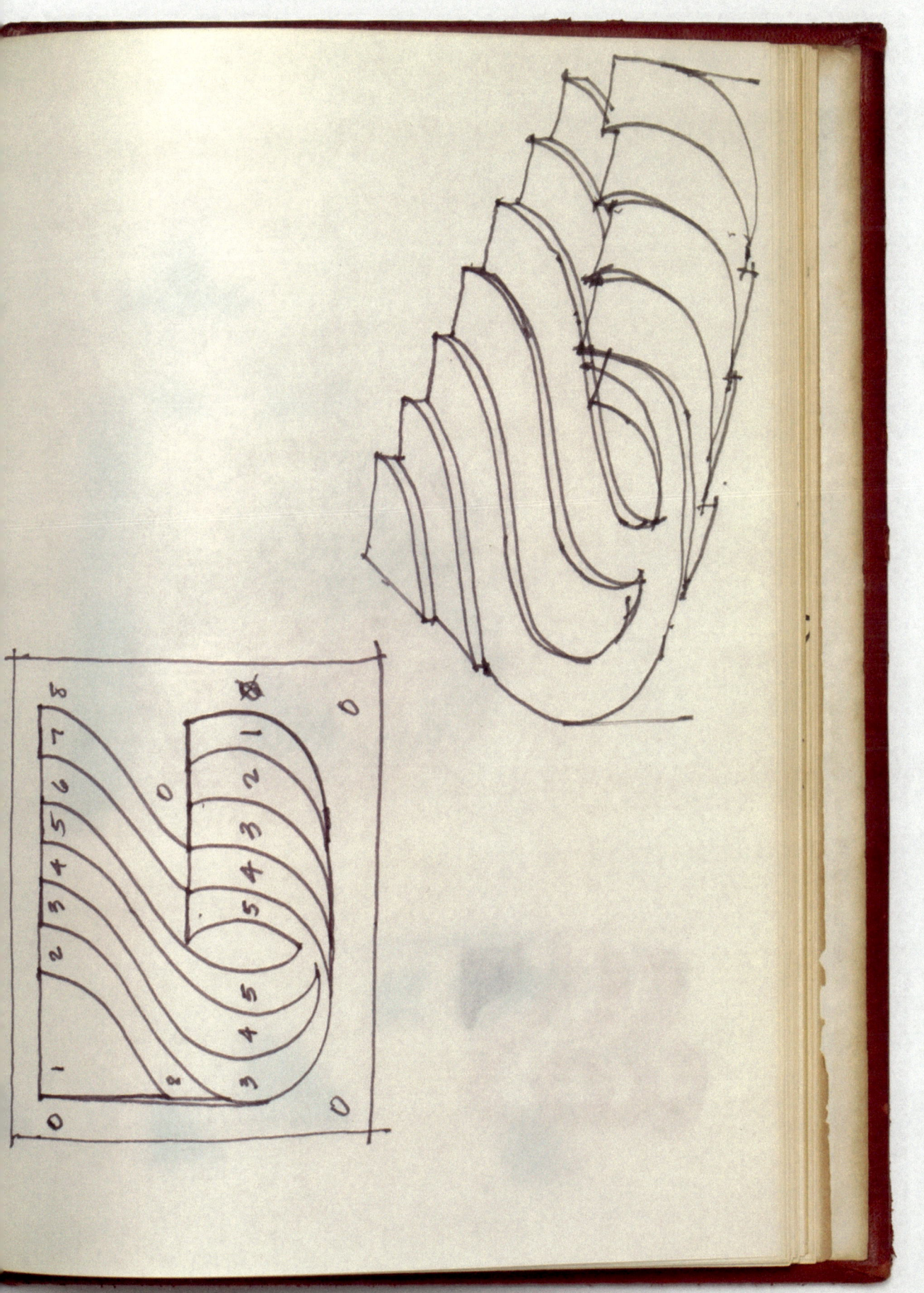

CELEBRATION OF THE MARDI GRAS

FOUR SEASONS
1 - SPRING
2 - SUMMER - JULY 4th
3 - FALL - HALLOWEEN
4 - WINTER { OLYMPICS, Xmas

HAPPY BIRTHDAY USA

SERVICE
1. PRESS

AT PYRAMIDS

FOUR SEASONS

1 - SPRING
2 - SUMMER - JULY 4TH
3 - FALL - HALLOWEEN
4 - WINTER < OLYMPICS, XMAS

SERVICE

1. PRESS

AT PYRAMIDS

IDENTIFICATION FOR GUIDES

VARIOUS LANGUAGES WOULD BE INDICATED BY THE INTERNATIONAL FLAGS

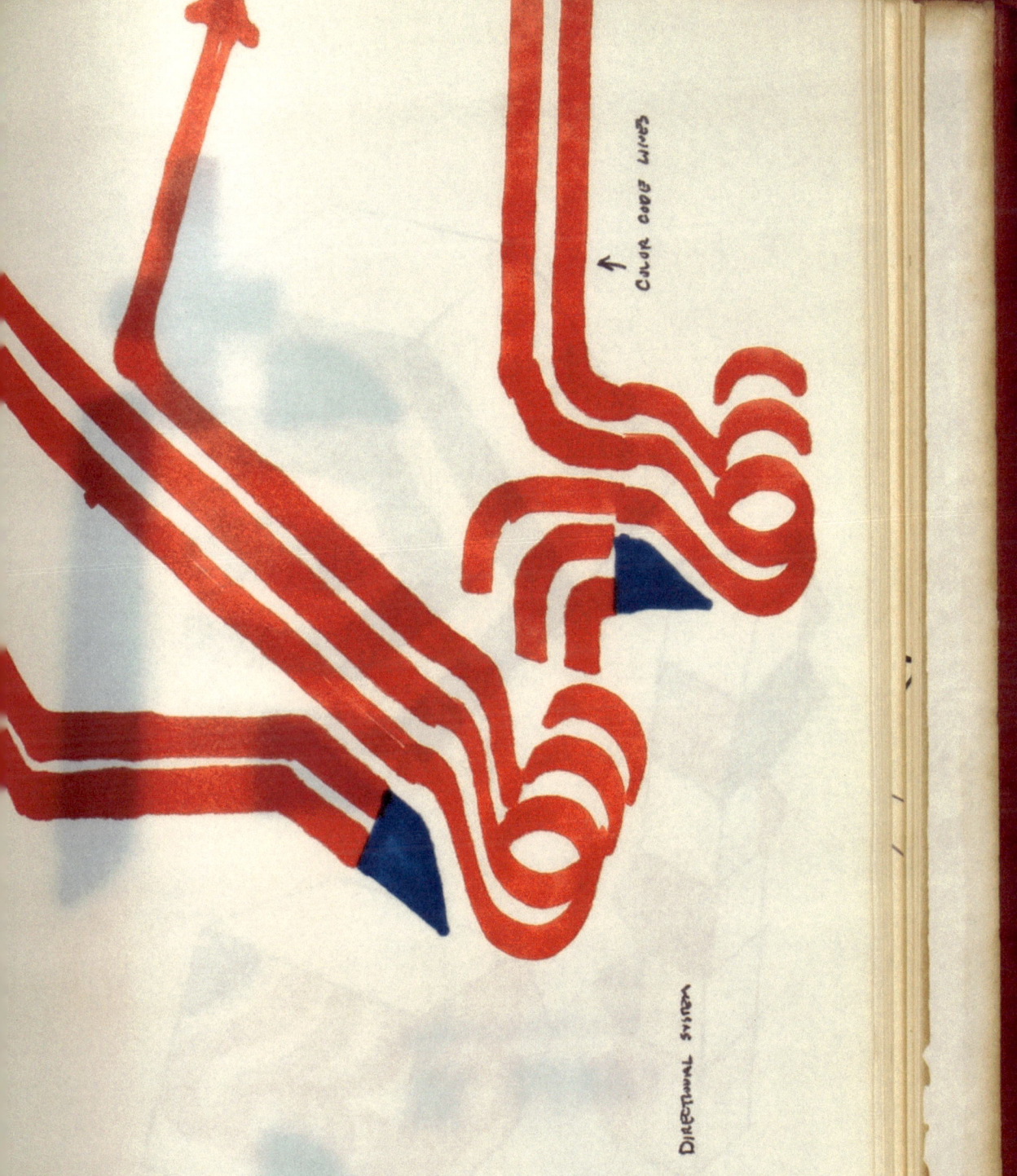

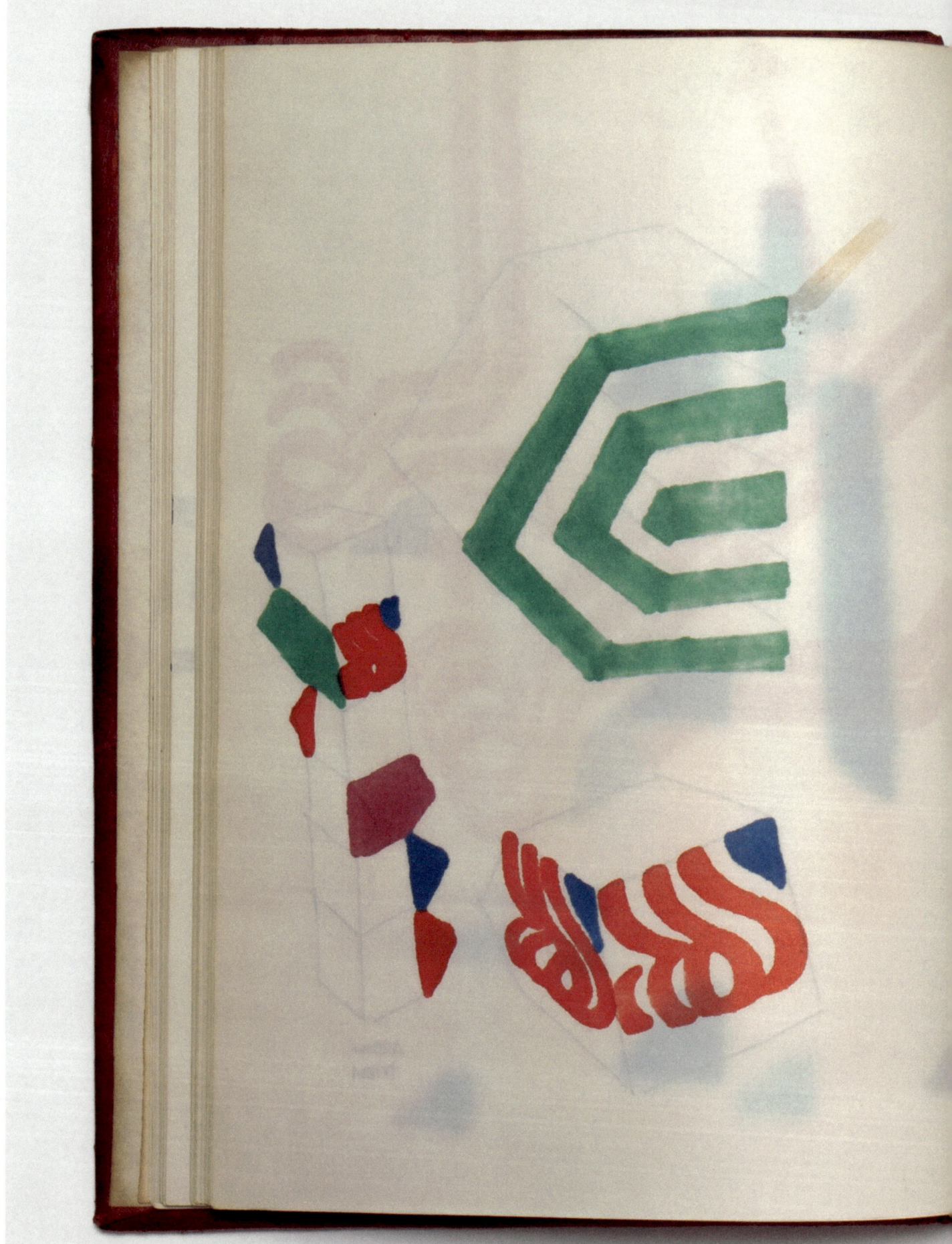

ABCDEFFGHIJ
KLLMNOPQ
UVWXorXYZ

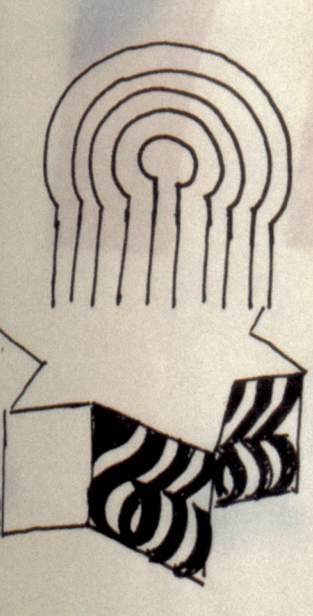
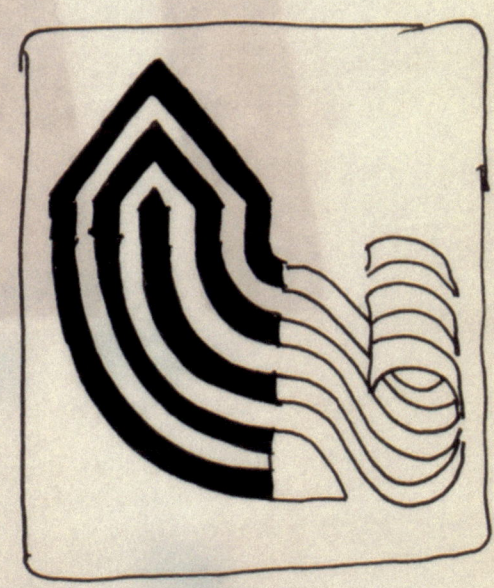

SEPT 10, 1970

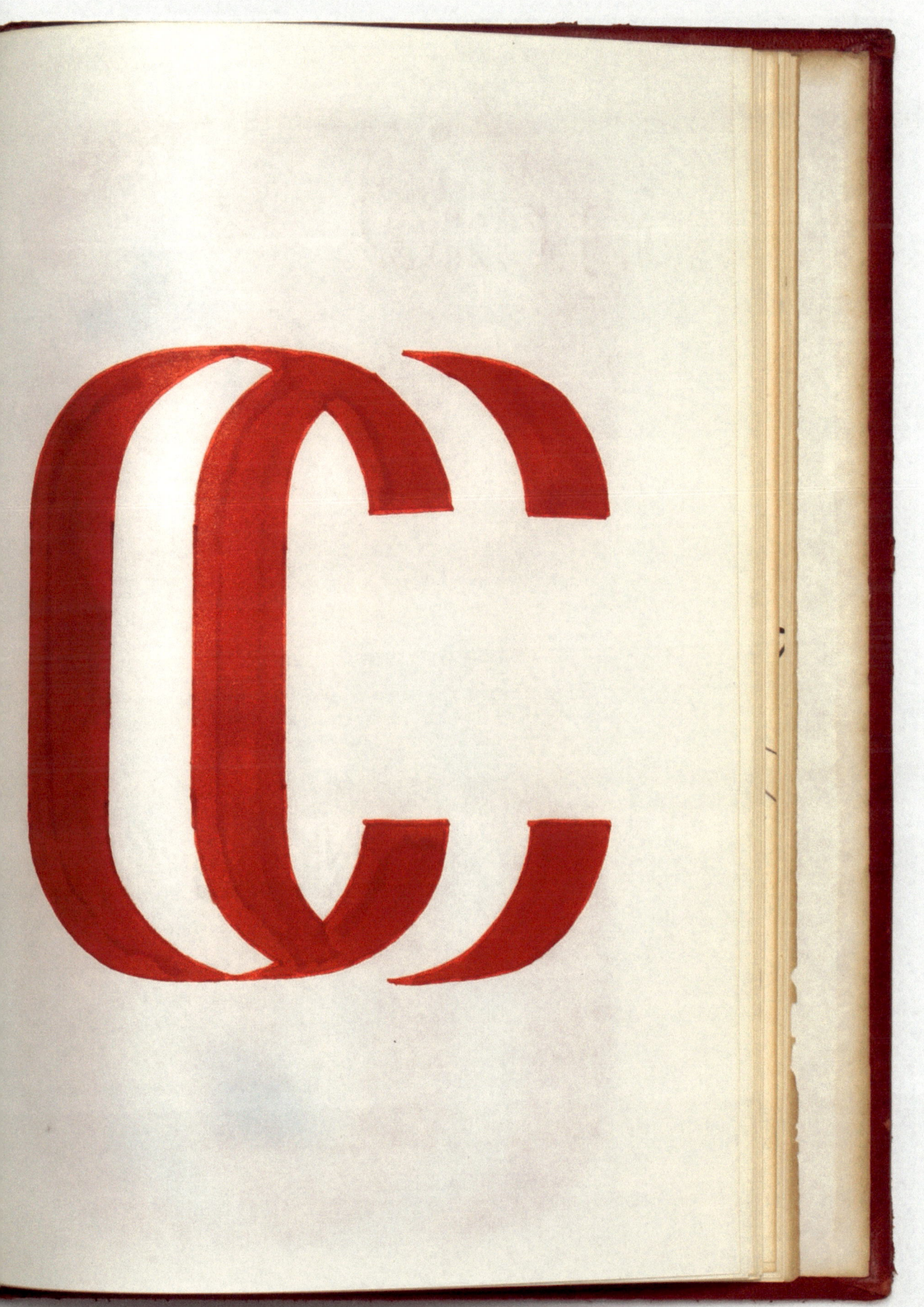

Philly

= COMMUNICATION
COME
COUNTER
CHILDREN

ENCLOSURE
GOOD SHAPE FOR SHELTER
OR PASSAGE
ASSEMBLY

= AMERICA
ARRIVAL
A (BEGIN)
ASCENT
AFTER

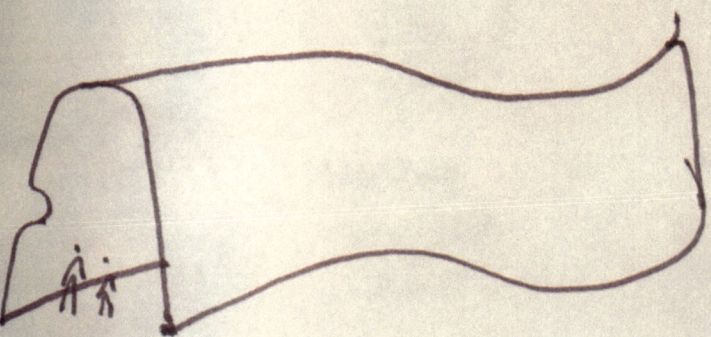

SHELTER OR
PASSAGE
SHAPE

= BOYS
BEGIN
BEFORE

COUNTER OR
PASSAGE, BOOTH

= COMMUNICATION
COME
COUNTER
CHILDREN

PASSAGE   = DESIGN
EXHIBIT   DESCRIPTION
                     DOGS
                     DOUGHNUT

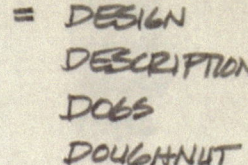

PASSAGE   = EMERGENCY
COUNTER   EXHIBIT
BOOTH   EXIT
                     ENTRANCE

COUNTER   = FOOD
SHELTER   FIRST
SHADE   FOUND
                     FINAL
                     FINISH

PASSAGE   = GOOD
SHELTER   GIFT
BOOTH ?   GIRLS

 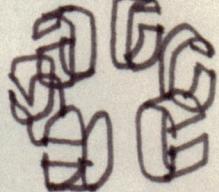

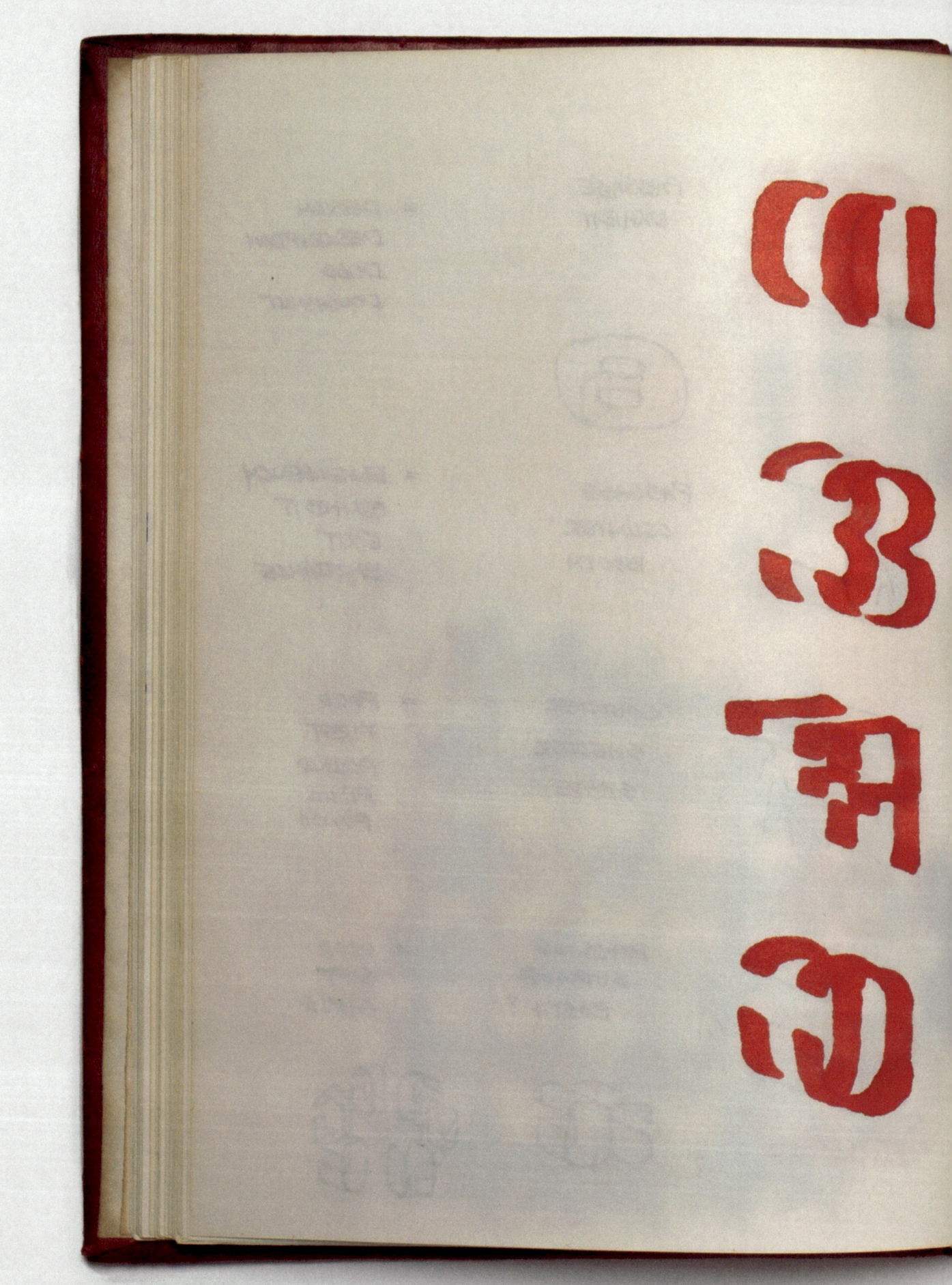

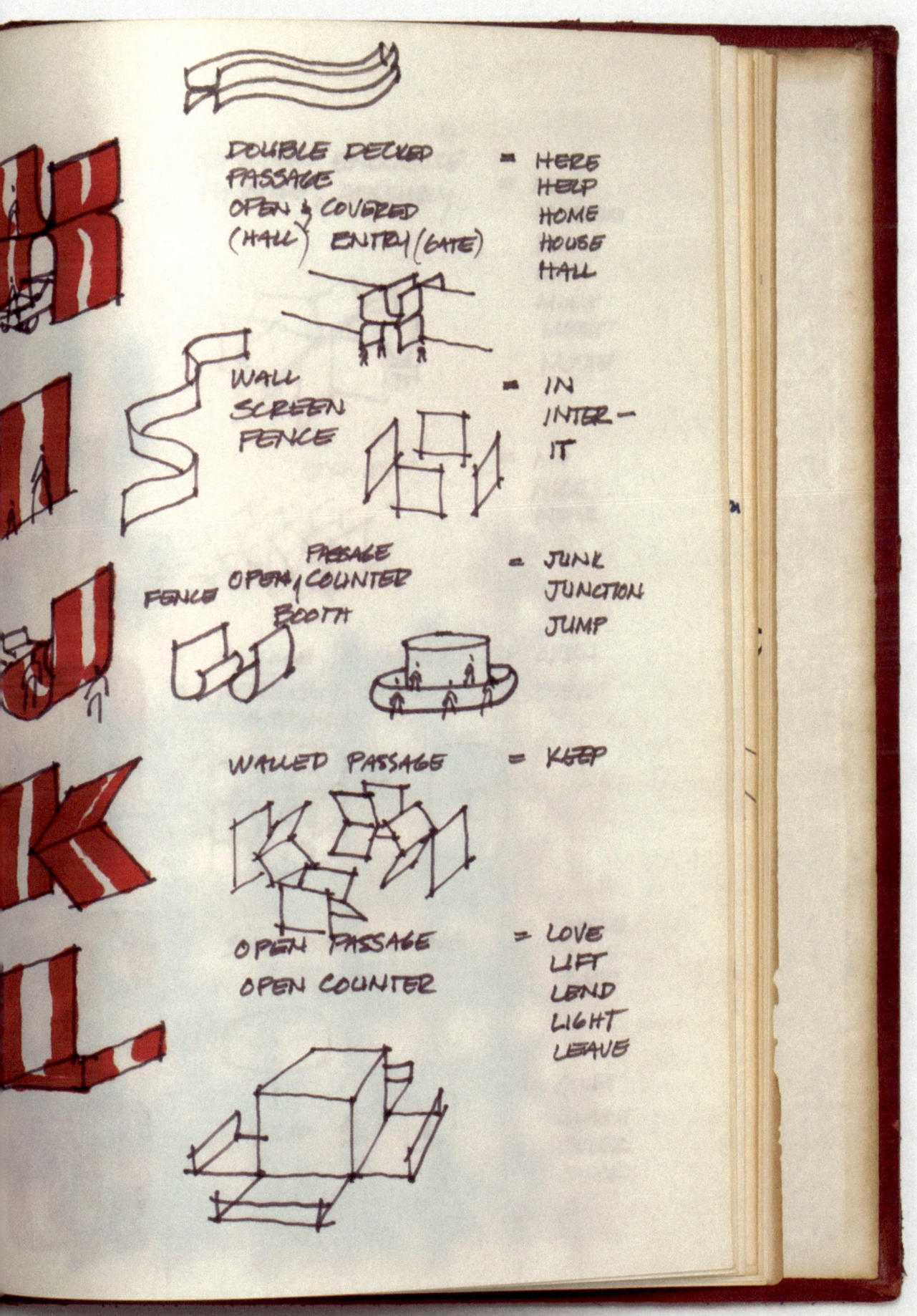

DOUBLE DECKED PASSAGE
OPEN & COVERED
(HALL) ENTRY (GATE)
= HERE
HELP
HOME
HOUSE
HALL

WALL
SCREEN
FENCE
= IN
INTER-
IT

FENCE PASSAGE
OPEN/COUNTER
BOOTH
= JUNK
JUNCTION
JUMP

WALLED PASSAGE
= KEEP

OPEN PASSAGE
OPEN COUNTER
= LOVE
LIFT
LEND
LIGHT
LEAVE

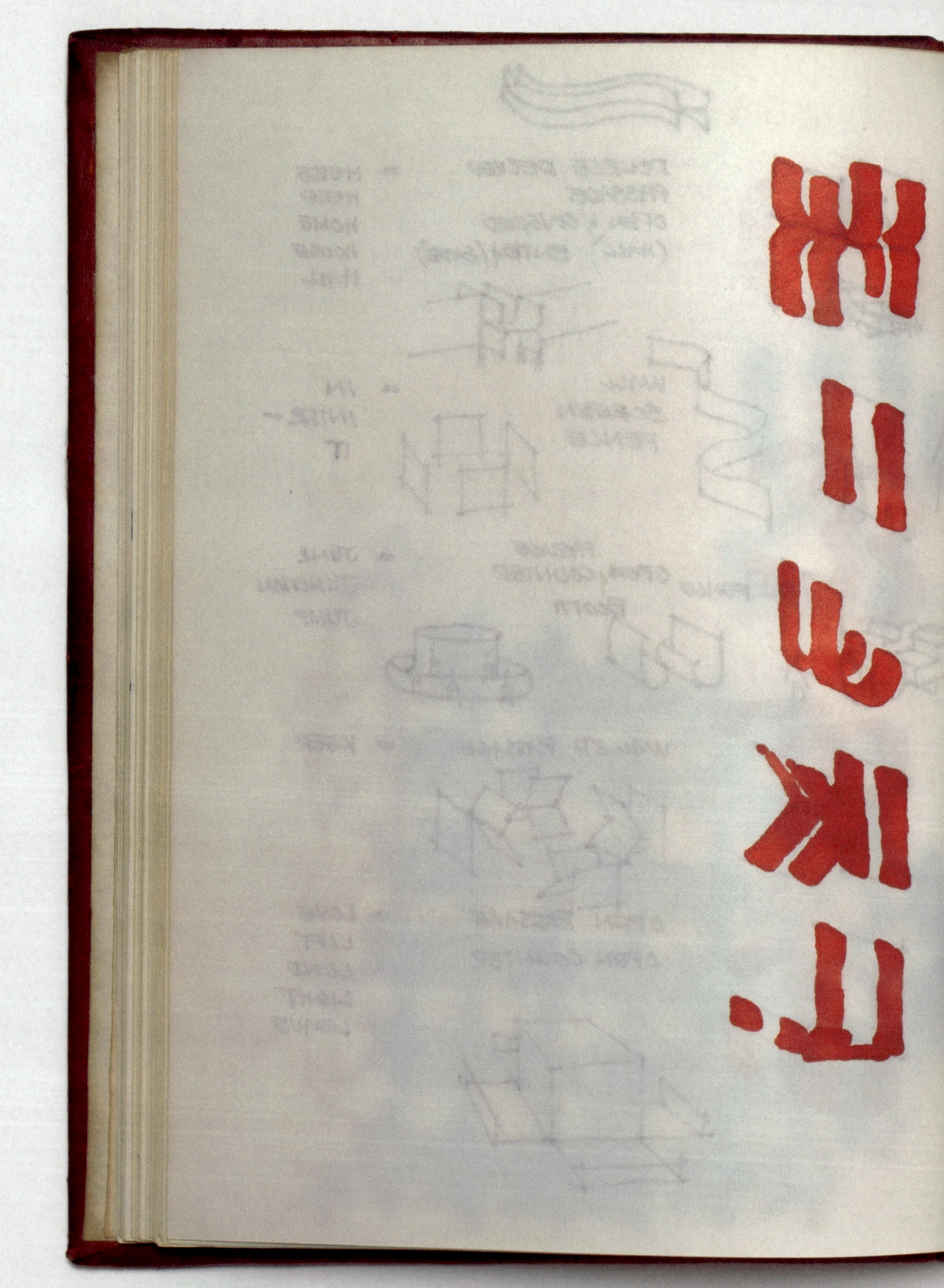

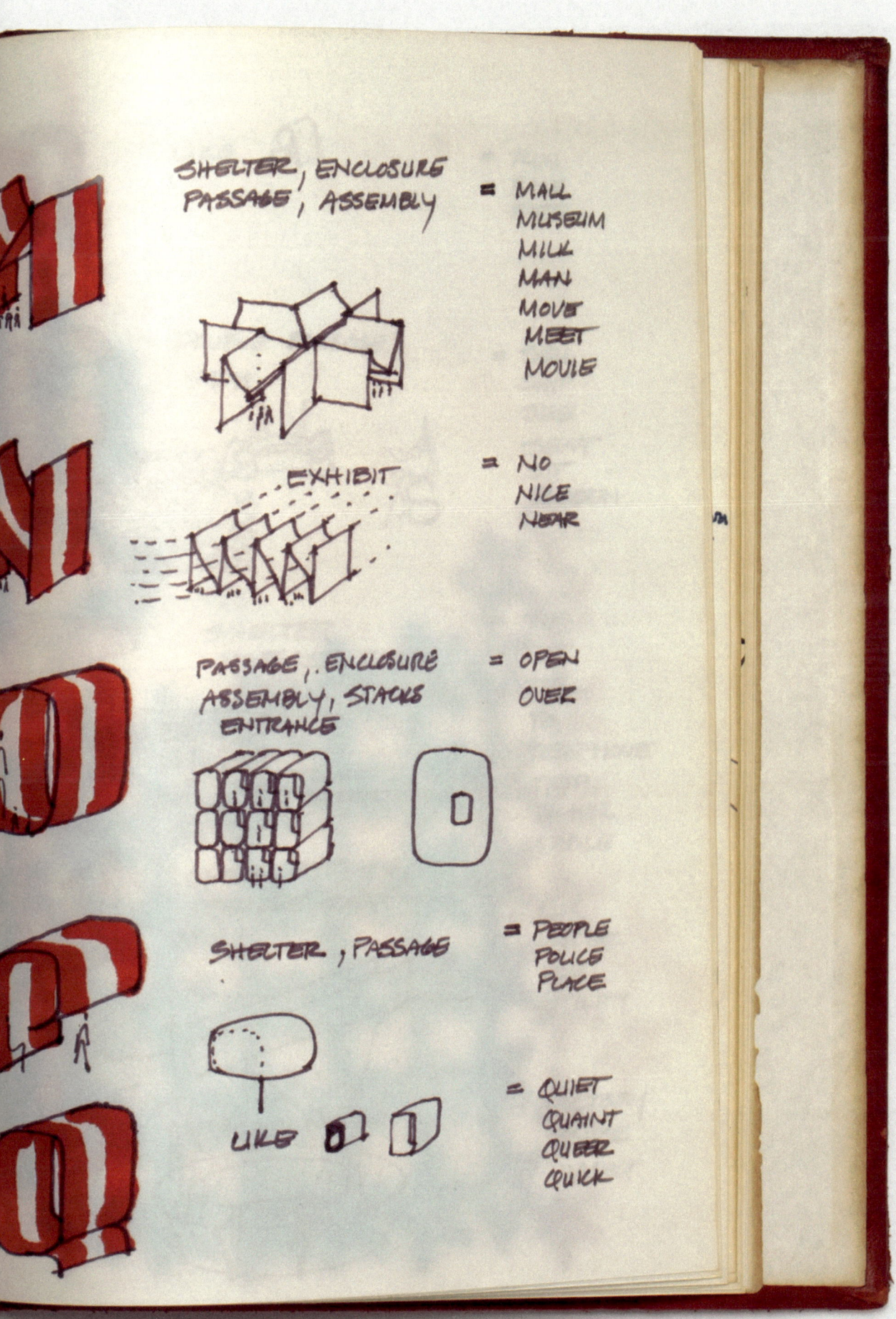

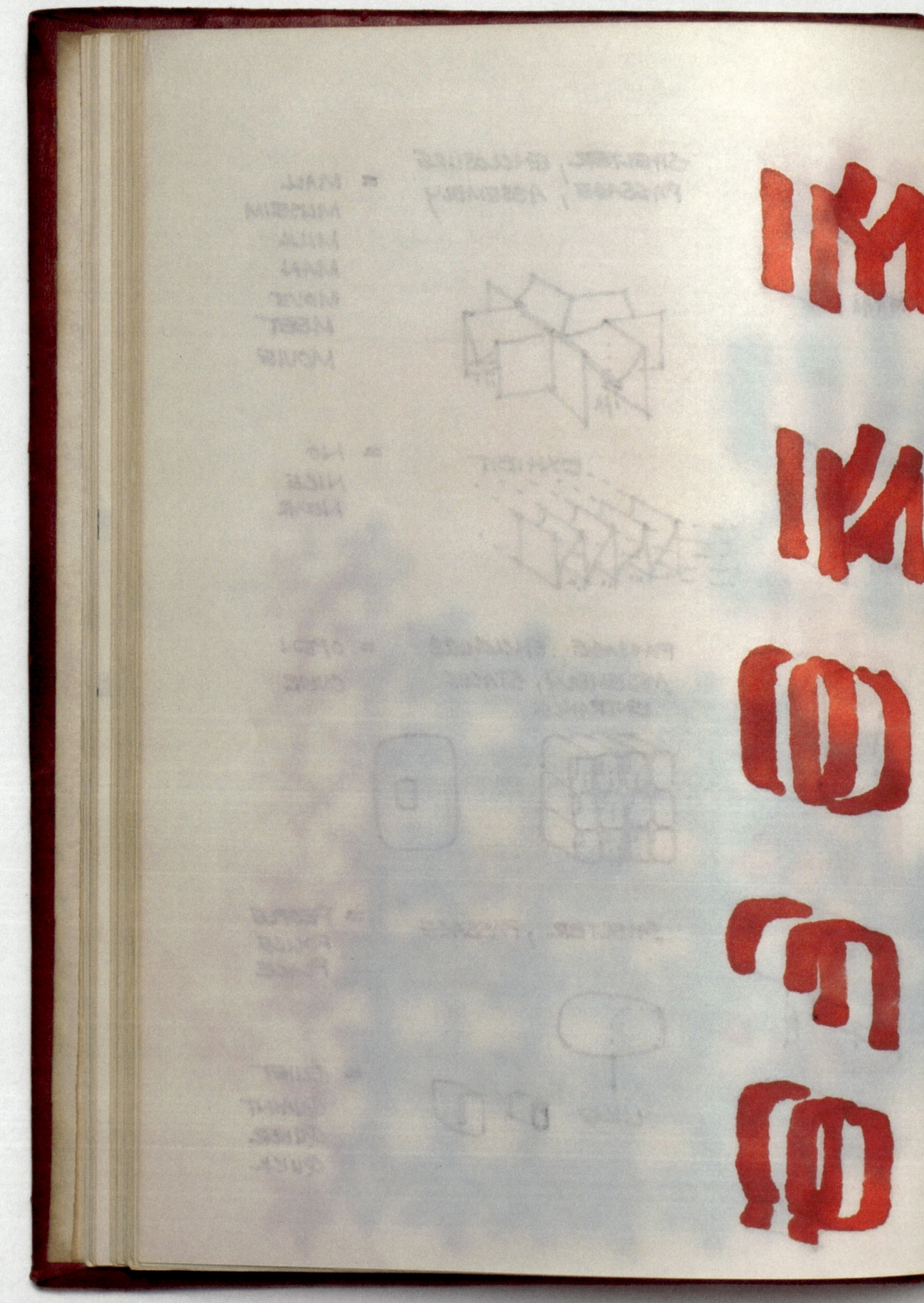

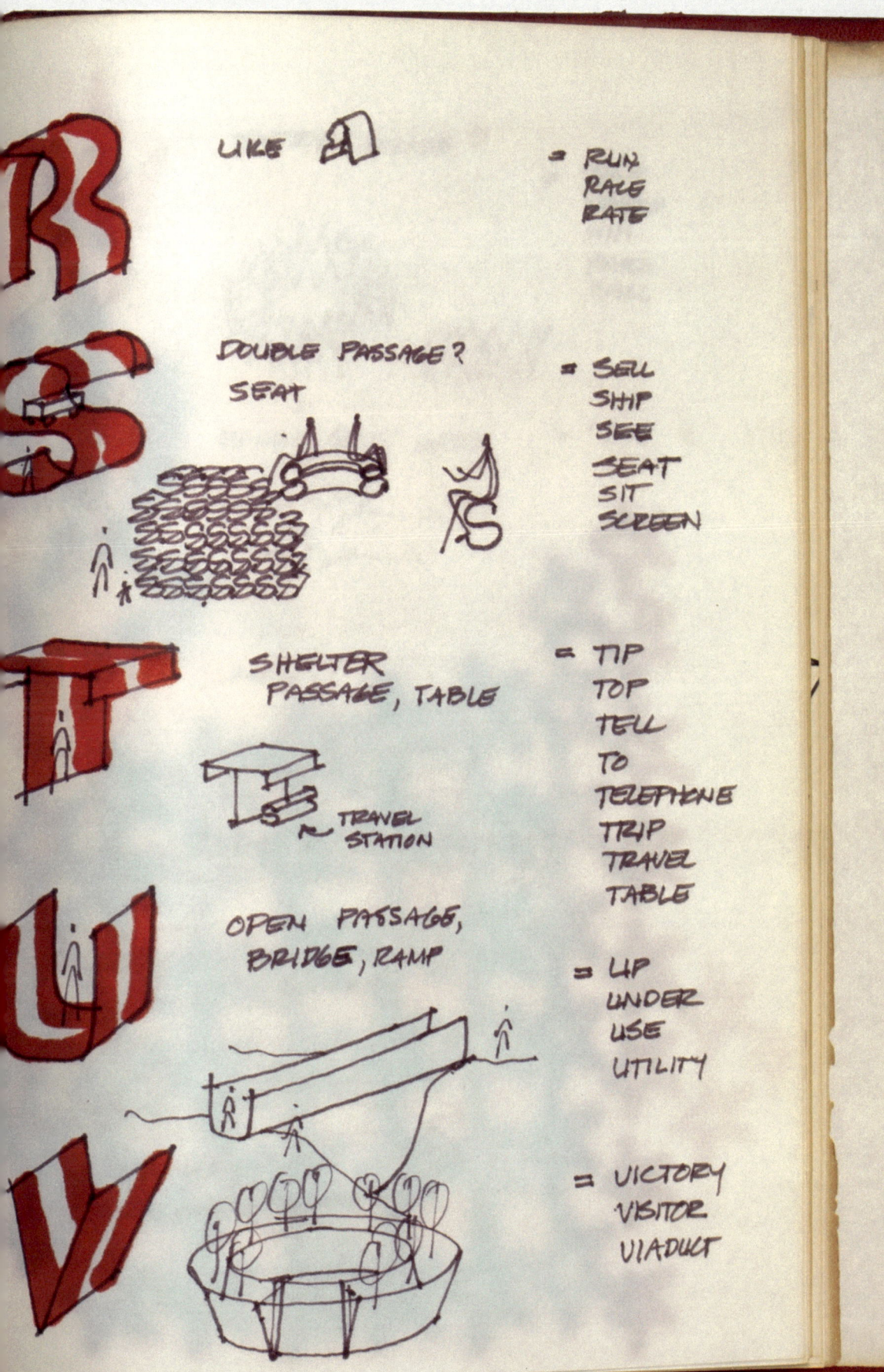

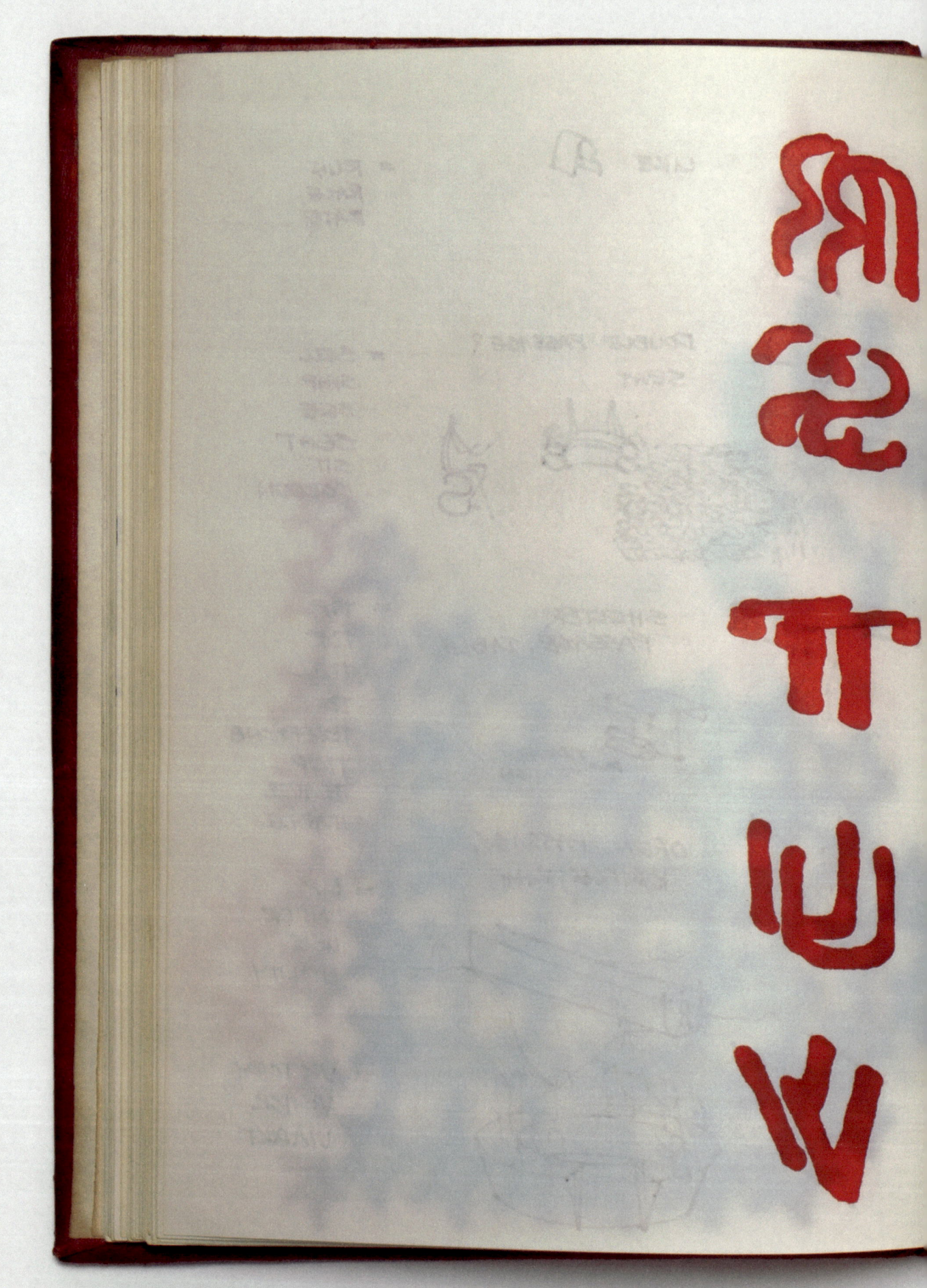

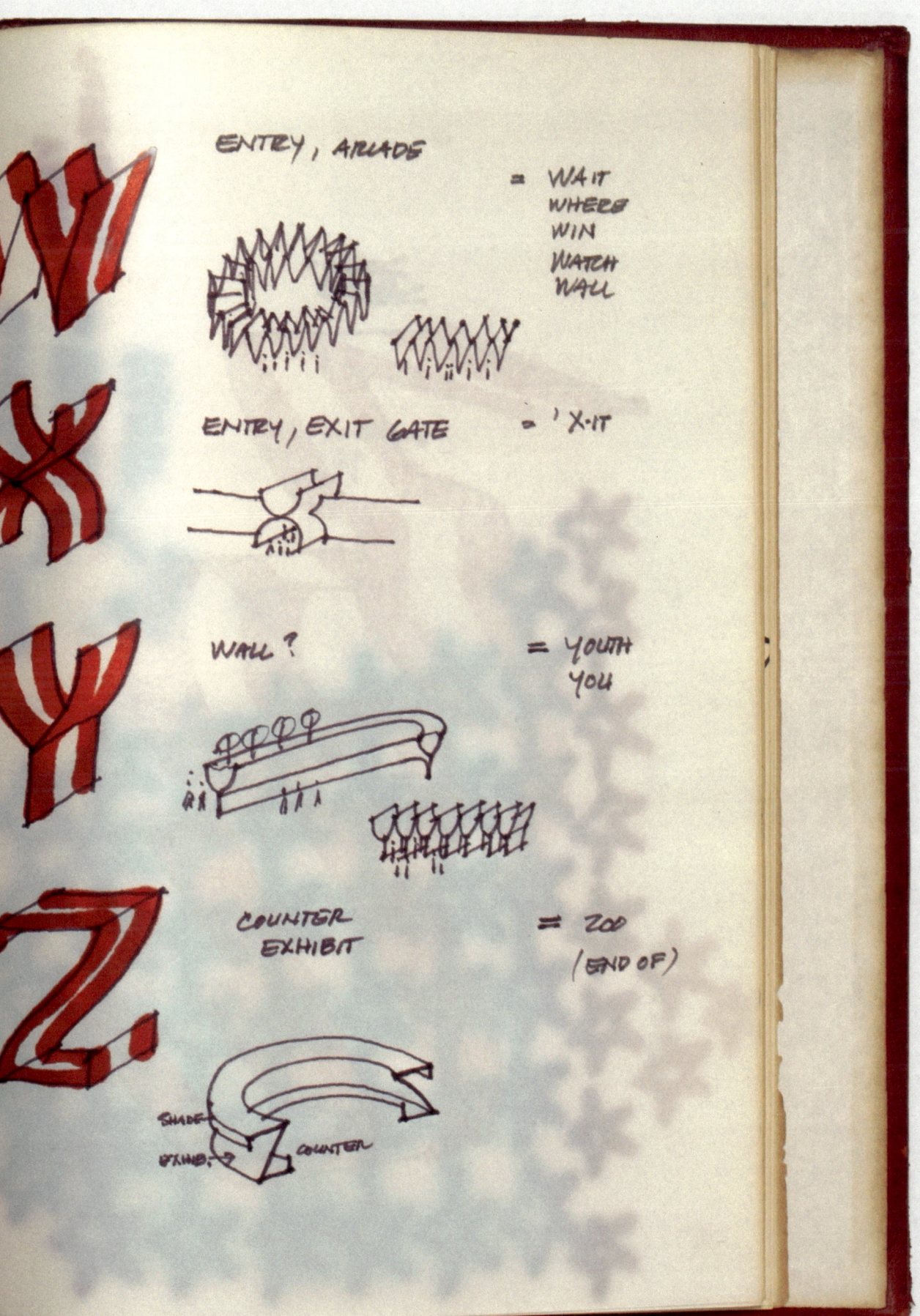

ENTRY, ARCADE = WAIT / WHERE / WIN / WATCH / WALL

ENTRY, EXIT GATE = 'X·IT

WALL? = YOUTH / YOU

COUNTER EXHIBIT = ZOO (END OF)

SHADE / EXHIB? / COUNTER

BUFFALO
EAGLE ← VERY IMPORTANT
↑ TORCH
↑ FLAG

SEPT 14, 1970

STAR FORMATIONS

EAGLE	OLYMPICS	PLANE
200	13 STATES (HERITAGE)	CAPITAL DOME (WASHINGTON)
TREE	WAGON WHEEL (HORIZONS)	WORLD
CANNON	CLIPPER SHIP	

① NEW SPIRIT FOR '76 (OVERALL SYMBOL)

② USA 200 →

→ THINK ORIGINAL IS STILL THE BEGINNING

HERITAGE '76 →

→ THINK WORLD

OPEN HOUSE USA →

→ THINK THE PATHS TO THE FUTURE

HORIZONS '76 →

WAGON WHEEL — START WITH EARLY PIONEERS

CHRISTMAS CARD

Star / State Canopy / Booth

Star Count of State Canopy / Wattho

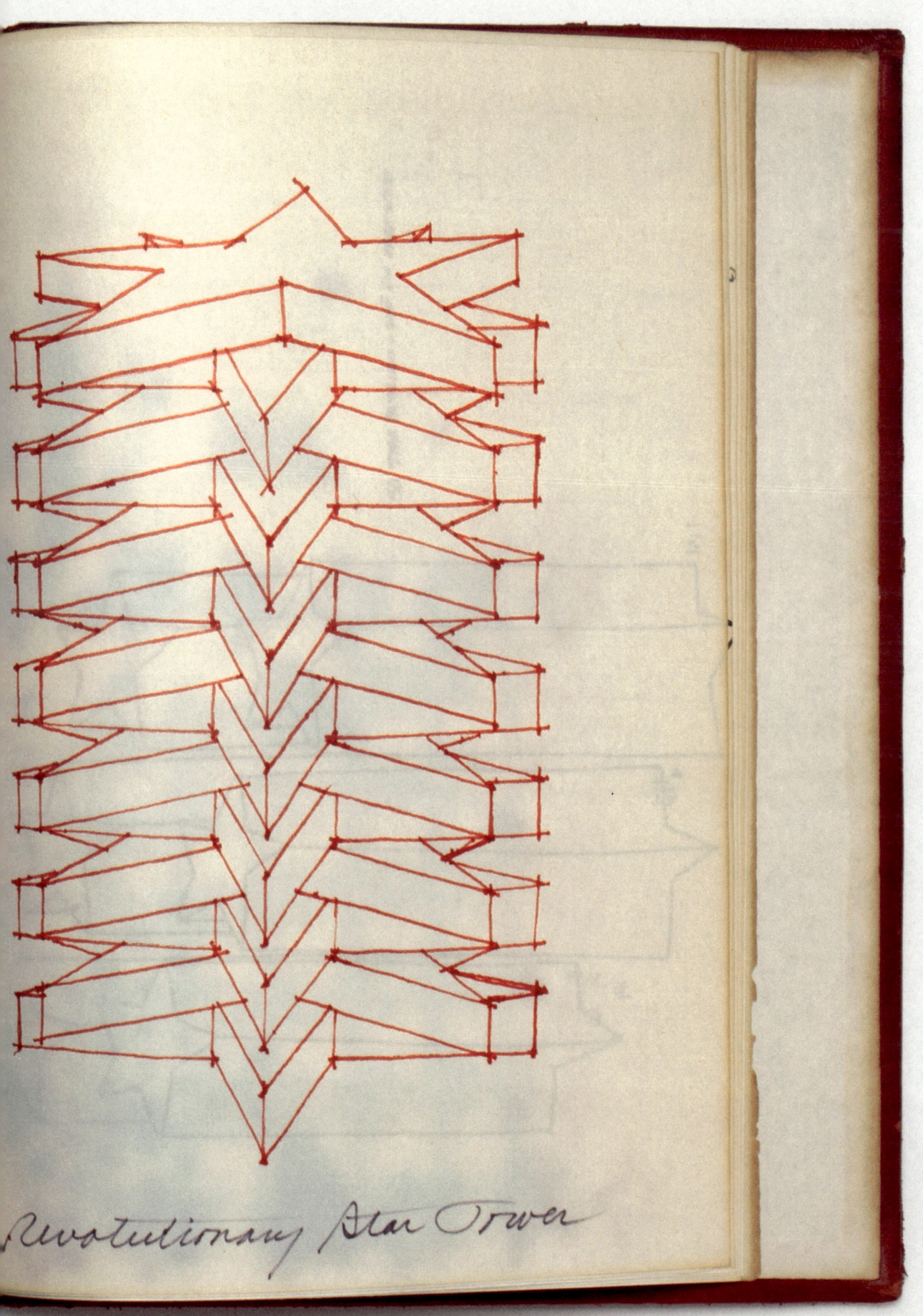

Revolutionary Star Tower

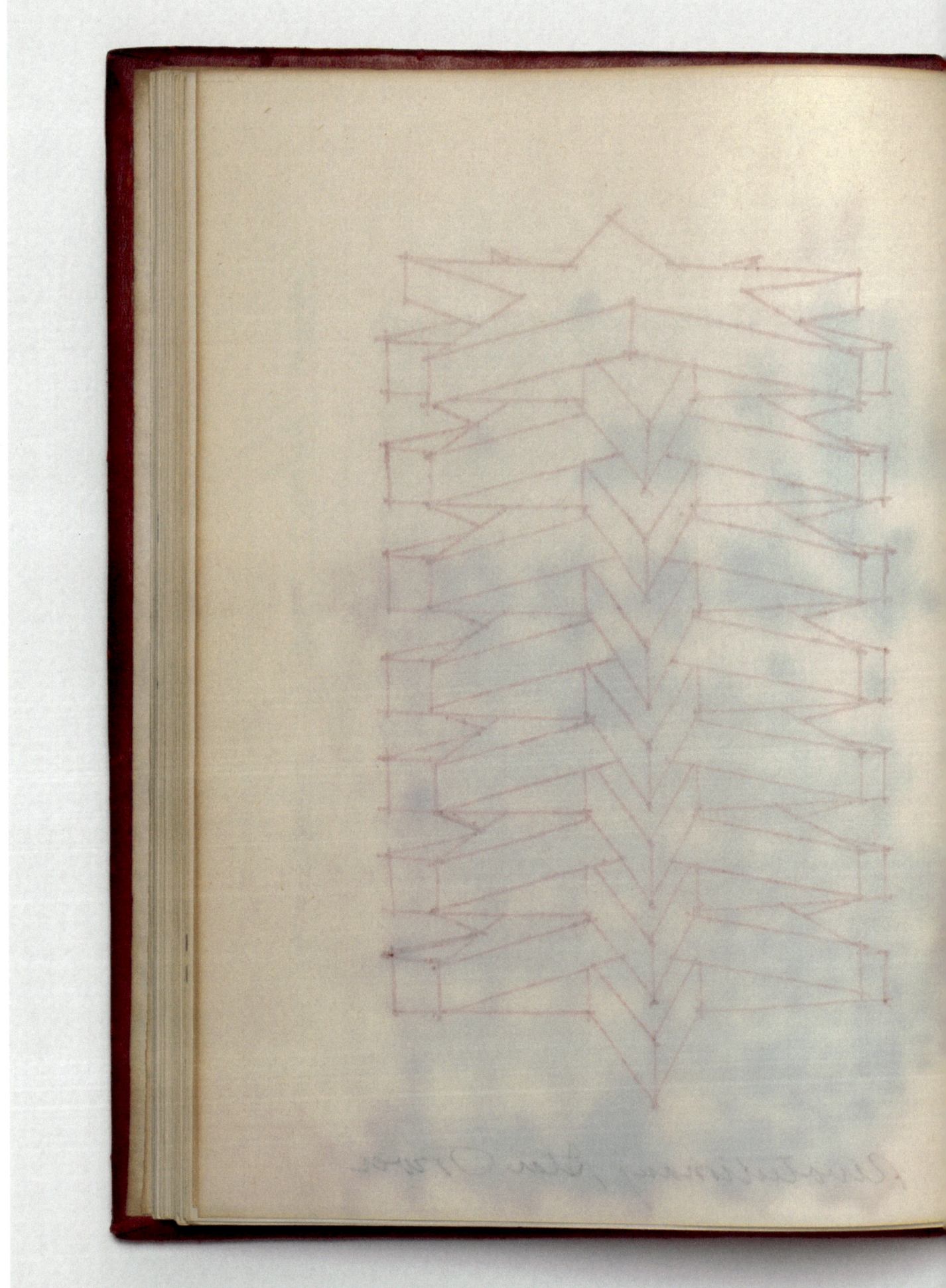

50 STAR PAVILIONS - ONE FOR EACH STATE

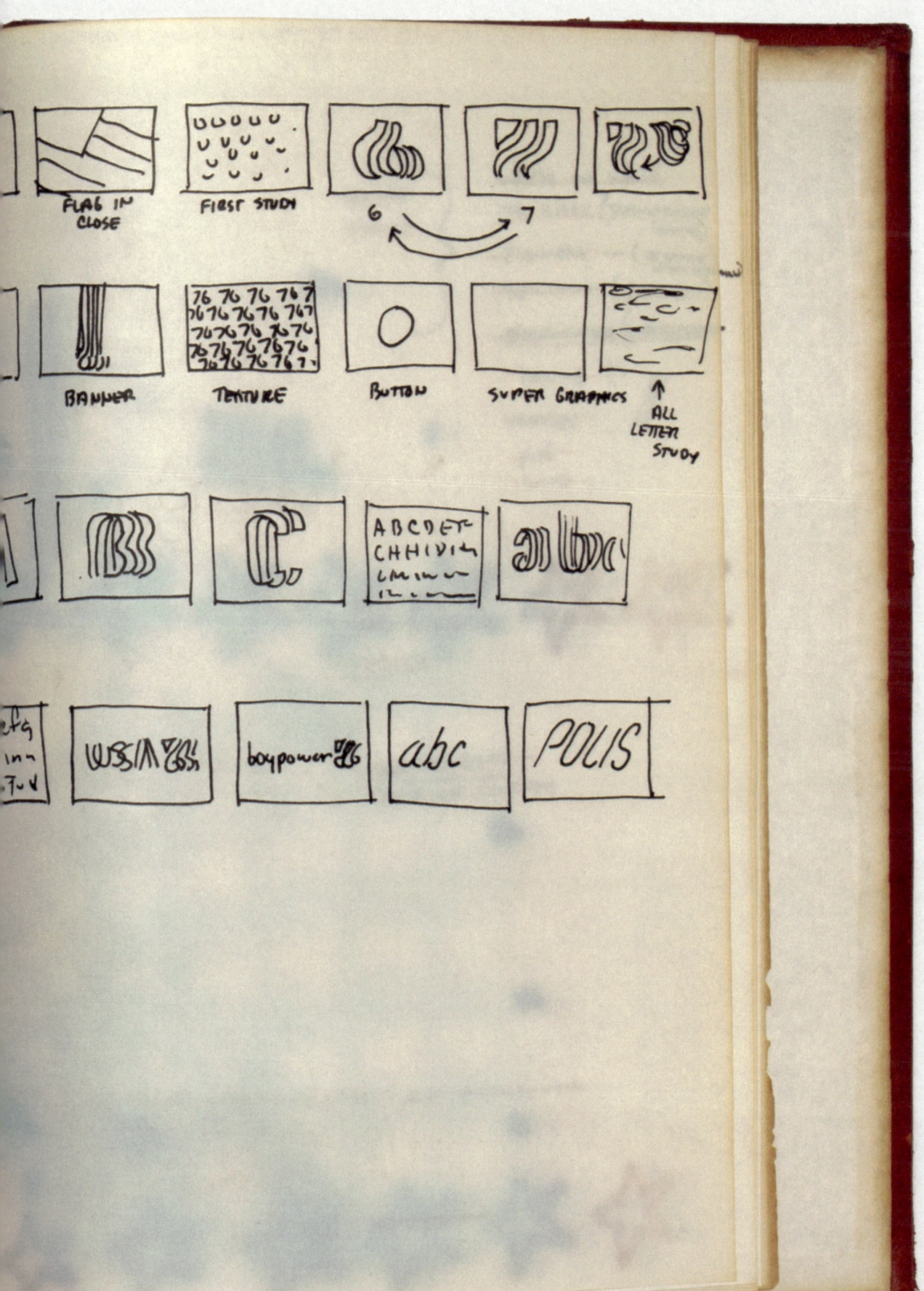

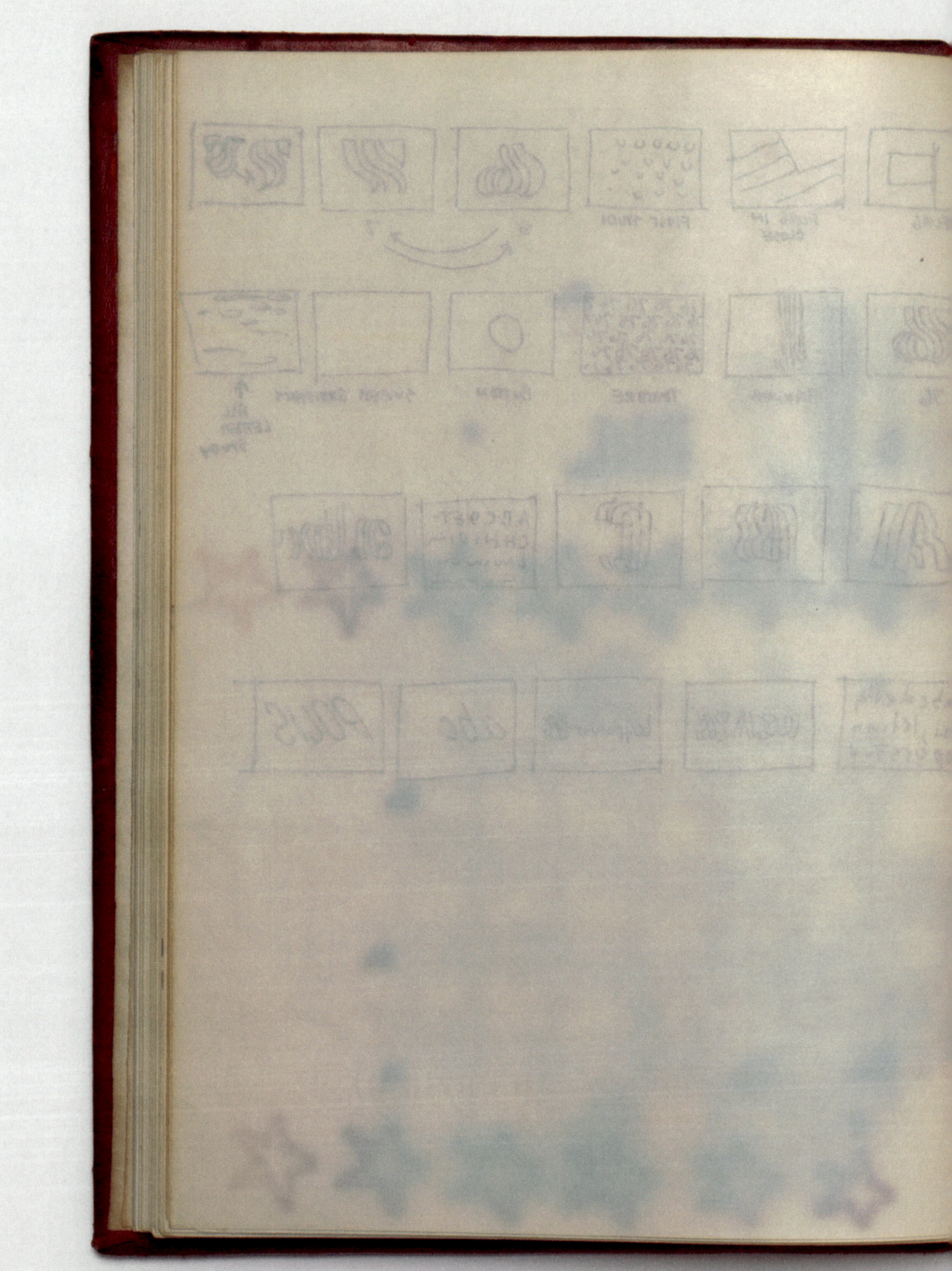

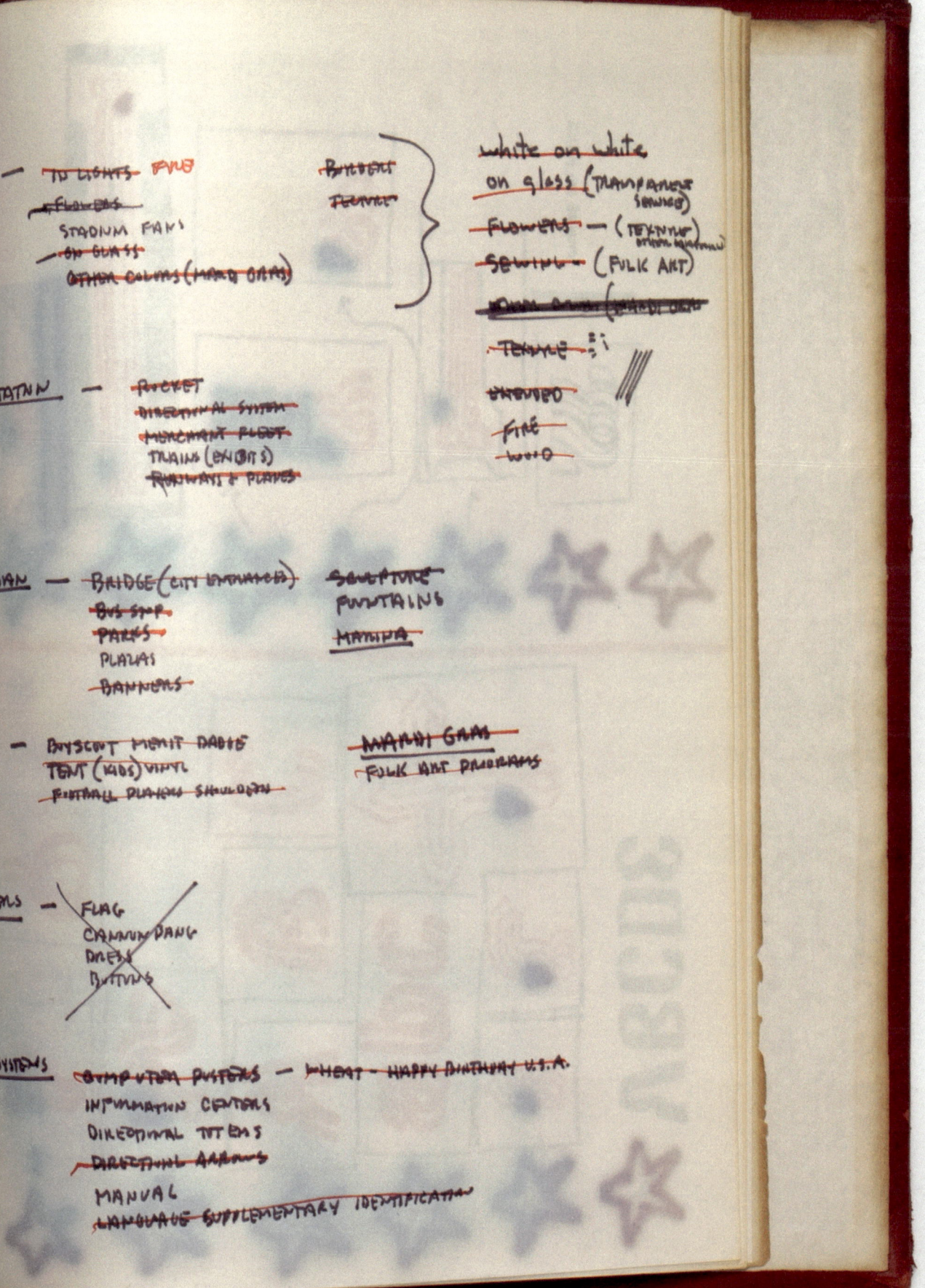

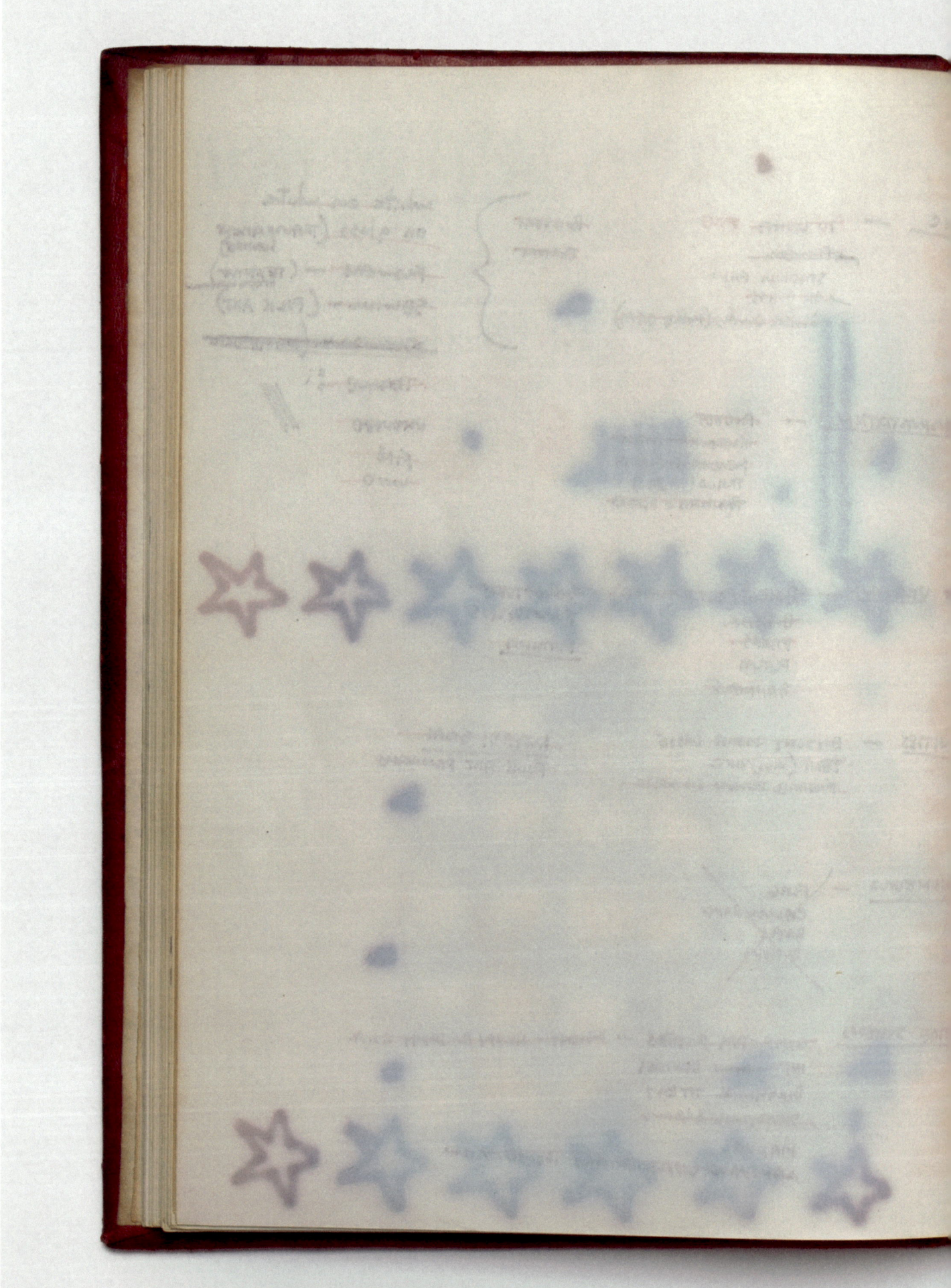

HAPPY BIRTHDAY U.S.A.

COMPUTER PRINTS EXAMPLE - FROM PROGRAM

USE THE NUMBER FROM 76

J	R	S
C	H	P
E	N	W
M	O	B
K	V	Z

ALPHABET OF LETTERS

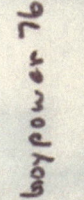
3-D LOGO

ABCDEFGHIJK LMNOPQRSTU VWXYZ

UPPER CASE

abcdefghijklm nopqrstuvwxyz

LOWER CASE

boy power 76

EXAMPLE OF LOWER CASE USE

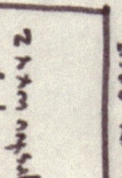
FIELD OF STARS FROM THE FINAL THE 50 STARS

NEW - NEW INTERPRETATION OF OVER USED SYMBOL

ABCDE ABCDE ABCDEFGHI ABCDEFGHI

OTHER TYPE FACES WORTH OF STUDIES

UPPER, LOWER & SYMBOL IN USE

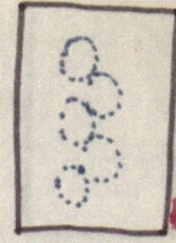
SIMPLIFIED VERSION DOWN UPGRADED

GAMES

OLYMPICS

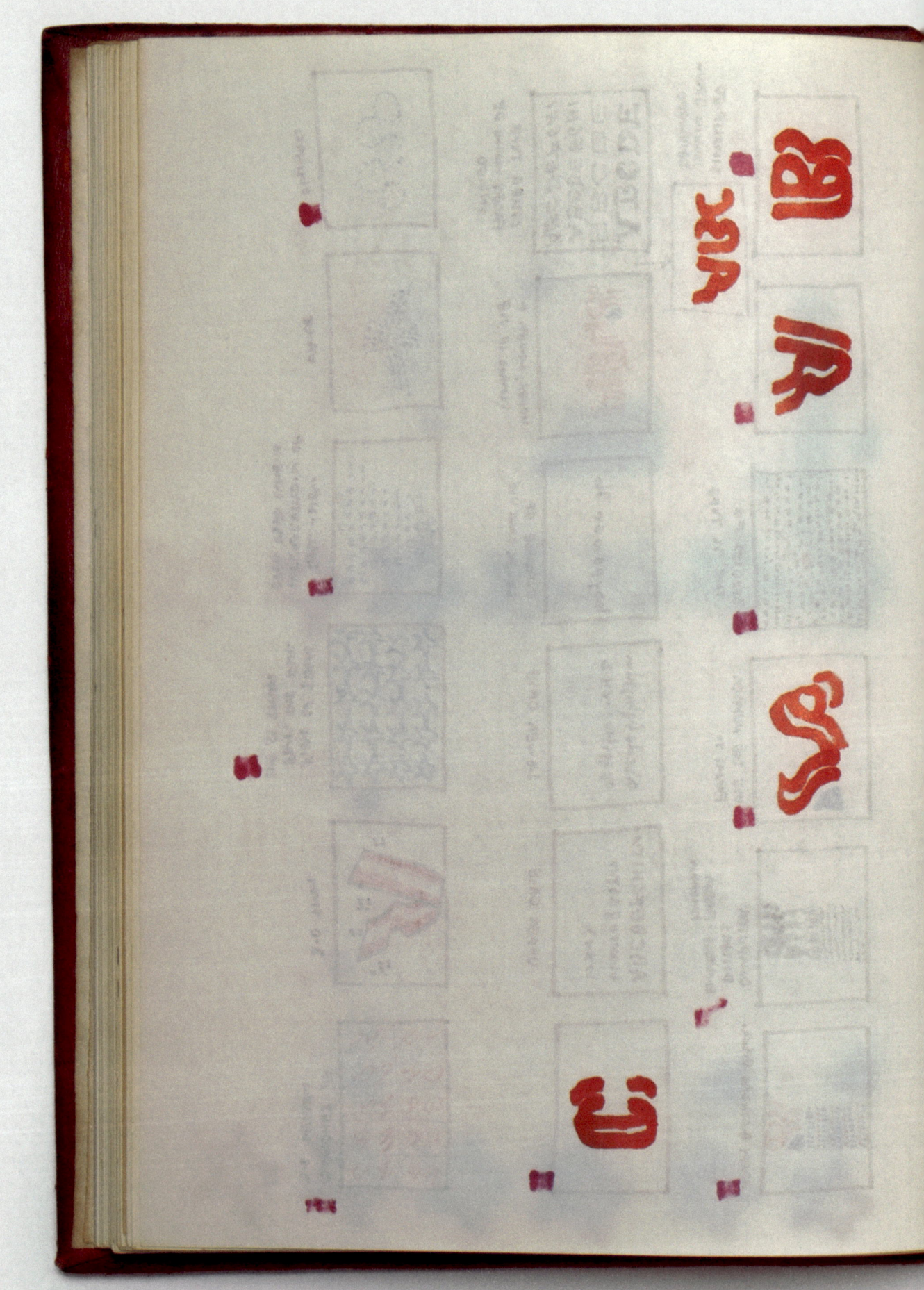

FNCB CAPITAL CORPORATION

A FEDERAL LICENSEE UNDER THE SMALL BUSINESS INVESTMENT ACT OF 1958

399 PARK AVENUE, NEW YORK, N. Y. 10022

August 17, 1970

Mr. Hugh A. Hall
Acting Executive Director
American Revolution Bicentennial Commission
Suite 319, Lafayette Building
811 Vermont Avenue, N. W.
Washington, D. C. 20242

Dear Mr. Hall:

Lance Wyman has asked me to confirm the financial responsibility and status of his design firm.

I have been closely involved with Mr. Wyman as both a banker and personal friend for several years. His business endeavors have proved to be very rewarding financially. I am personally involved with administering his domestic estate and business activities of which his personal net worth is presently in the upper five figures.

I have no doubts as to Mr. Wyman's financial stability and ability to deliver any major project that his firm undertakes.

If I can be of any further assistance, please do not hesitate to call upon me.

Sincerely,

G. Ronald Millican
Assistant Treasurer

COMPREHENSIVE DESIGN AND GRAPHICS PROGRAM FOR THE OFFICIAL COMMEMORATION OF THE BICENTENNIAL OF THE UNITED STATES

PRESIDENT NIXON STATED, REGARDING THE OVERALL BICENTENNIAL THEME, " . . . THIS EVENT WILL BE FESTIVE, COLORFUL AND AFFIRMATIVE; YET IT MUST ALSO BE THOUGHTFUL, PROFOUND AND SEARCHING."

THE DESIGN AND GRAPHICS PROGRAM SHOULD BE ABLE TO ENCOMPASS THESE SYMBOLIC REQUIREMENTS.

THIS CAN BE DONE BY FIRST DEVELOPING A SYMBOLIC LOGO.

THE LOGO SHOULD DICTATE AND BE PART OF AN OVERALL SYSTEM OF DESIGN THAT WILL STIMULATE PEOPLE TO MAKE THEIR OWN EFFORT TO WANT TO BECOME INVOLVED AND WANT TO CONTRIBUTE IN A POSITIVE WAY TO THE BICENTENNIAL THEME.

THE FOLLOWING PROPOSAL PRESENTS A SERIES OF IDEAS TO ACHIEVE THIS GOAL:

SLIDE #	COMMENT
1.	OUR NATION WAS BORN IN 1776. 1976 WILL BE THE FOCAL POINT FOR OUR BICENTENNIAL CELEBRATION
2.	THE UNITED STATES FLAG OUR FLAG SYMBOLIZES THE NATION.
3.	GRAPHIC STUDIES BASED ON THE VISUAL ELEMENTS OF THE FLAG AND THE YEAR '76.
4.	A WIND BLOWN FLAG THE CHARACTER OF THE WIND BLOWN FLAG SUGGESTED MANY VISUAL FORMS.
5.	THE NUMBER 7. BY CONTROLLING THESE FORMS, THEY CAN VISUALLY EXPRESS IDEAS.
6.	THE NUMBER 6. THIS CONTROL MAKES IT POSSIBLE TO DEVELOP THE NUMBERS 7 & 6.

DESIGN PROGRAM – PAGE TWO

SLIDE #	COMMENT
7.	COMBINING THE 7 & 6 BY COMBINING THE 7 & 6, THE YEAR OF THE BICENTENNIAL CELEBRATION IS DEFINED.
8.	THE COMBINED 76 A LOGO POSSIBILITY, VISUALLY RELATED TO OUR FLAG, GRAPHI-CALLY GIVING FORM TO THE SPIRIT AND ASPIRATIONS OF OUR '76 CELEBRATION.
9.	LOGO IN BAS RELIEF THE LOGO CAN BE UTILIZED IN MANY DIFFERENT FORMS. EMBOSSING COULD BE USED FOR LETTERHEADS, BAS RELIEF CAN BE USED IN ARCHITECTURAL APPLICATIONS, ETC.
10.	LOGO ON A TRANSPARENT SURFACE.
11.	FLAME APPLICATION OF LOGO. THE LOGO CAN BE INTEGRATED WITH APPROPRIATE CEREMONIAL APPLICATIONS, THE WINTER OLYMPICS, EDUCATIONAL PROGRAMS
12.	THE LOGO WORN AS A PENDANT THE LOGO CAN BE FORMED IN MANY DIFFERENT SCALES IN METAL.
13.	THE LOGO EMBROIDERED CRAFTS PEOPLE CAN PARTICIPATE IN APPLYING THE LOGO.
14.	THE LOGO IN WOOD.
15.	GEORGE WASHINGTON CROSSING THE DELAWARE IN THE LOGO. THE LOGO CAN BE COMBINED WITH PICTORIAL INFORMATION.
16.	SPACE PHOTO IN THE LOGO.
17.	LOGO ON MAP. THE LOGO CAN BE USED TO IDENTIFY ALL MATERIAL OFFICIALLY RELATED TO THE PROGRAM.
18.	TWO LOGOS IN DIFFERENT COLORS. THE LOGO CAN BE USED IN DIFFERENT COLORS TO RELATE IT TO SPECIFIC EVENTS: THE MARDI GRAS, ETC.
19.	TEXTURE OF LOGOS THE LOGO ADAPTS TO DECORATIVE APPLICATIONS SUCH AS BORDERS AND TEXTURES.
20.	THE LOGO EXTENDED VERTICALLY THE DESIGN OF THE LOGO ALLOWS IT TO EXTEND VERTICALLY.
21.	THE AIR STRIP THE LOGO CAN SERVE AS A WELCOME AT THE NATION'S GATEWAYS.
22.	THE BRIDGE.
23.	LOGO APPLIED TO BACK OF BUS STOP.

DESIGN PROGRAM - PAGE THREE

SLIDE #   COMMENT

24.   SIDE VIEW OF BUS STOP.

25.   TOP VIEW OF BUS STOP.

26.   FRONT VIEW OF BUS STOP.
        THE COLORED AREAS ON THE FRONT WOULD BE SPECIFIC INFORM-
        ATION RELATED TO THE TRANSPORTATION ROUTES.

27.   CLOSE-UP OF PARK
        PART OF CELEBRATION COULD BE THE CREATION OF NEW PARK SPACES
        IN OUR TOWNS AND CITIES.

28.   AERIAL VIEW OF PARK
        THE LOGO COULD BE USED AS A SYMBOLIC FUNCTIONAL FORM FOR
        PARKS AND PLAZAS.

29.   SIDE VIEW OF THREE DIMENSIONAL LOGO
        THREE DIMENSIONAL STRUCTURES COULD BE BUILT TO SERVE AS
        PARK SCULPTURE OR AS ENTRANCES TO ARCHITECTURAL SPACE.

30.   AERIAL VIEW OF THREE DIMENSIONAL LOGO FROM BOTTOM SIDE.

31.   AERIAL VIEW OF THREE DIMENSIONAL LOGO FROM TOP SIDE.

32.   LOGO IN THE FORM OF STAIRS.
        THE LOGO CAN ADAPT TO THE FUNCTIONAL FORM OF A STAIRWELL.

33.   STAIRWELL WITH A TRANSPARENT CANOPY.

34.   A MARINA
        MARINAS COULD BE BUILT FOR RECREATIONAL USE AND FOR WATER
        SPORT EVENTS.

35.   FOOTBALL PLAYER
        THE NATION'S PROFESSIONAL SPORTSMEN COULD PARTICIPATE IN THE
        CELEBRATION.

36.   LOGO IN FLOWERS.
        THE SPORTING PROGRAMS OF THE NATION'S COLLEGES AND UNIVER-
        SITIES WOULD BE PART OF THE CELEBRATION: ROSE BOWL.

37.   SKIIER
        THE LOGO COULD BE INTEGRATED WITH THE '76 WINTER OLYMPICS

38.   BOYSCOUT MERIT BADGE
        THE NATION'S YOUTH ORGANIZATIONS COULD GIVE SPECIAL AWARDS
        FOR '76 ACHIEVEMENTS.

39.   TRANSPARENT TENT
        THE LOGO COULD BE INTEGRATED IN OTHER WAYS WITH YOUNG PEOPLES'
        ACTIVITIES.

DESIGN PROGRAM - PAGE FOUR

SLIDE #	COMMENT
40.	BABY WITH '76 T-SHIRT
41.	CANNON WITH LOGO BANNER THE LOGO COULD BE PART OF SOUVENIR PROGRAMS.
42.	LOGO AT MEXICAN PYRAMID. THE SPIRIT OF THE '76 CELEBRATION WOULD BE CARRIED TO ALL PARTS OF THE WORLD BY TRAVELING AMERICANS.
43.	LOGO ON SIDE OF SHIP. CARRIED BY NATION'S MERCHANT FLEET.
44.	LOGO ON AIRLINER IT COULD BE CARRIED BY THE AIR FLEET.
45.	LOGO ON ROCKET. IT COULD BE CARRIED INTO SPACE.
46.	7 & 6 SEPARATING THE CHARACTER OF THE NUMBERS WHICH ARE COMBINED TO MAKE THE LOGO CAN BE UTILIZED TO CREATE A COMPLETE ALPHABET.
47.	STUDIES OF THE ALPHABET. WE MADE MANY STUDIES SO THAT THE LETTERS OF THE ALPHABET COULD BE DEVELOPED.
48.	THE LETTER A
49.	THE LETTER B
50.	THE LETTER C
51.	THE '76 TYPEFACE AT THIS POINT OF REFINEMENT, THE TYPEFACE CONTAINS AN UPPER CASE ALPHABET, A LOWER CASE ALPHABET AND NUMERALS.
52.	BOYPOWER '76 EXAMPLE OF THE LOWER CASE ALPHABET IN USE.
53.	ARBC '76 EXAMPLE OF THE UPPER CASE ALPHABET IN USE.
54.	SKETCHES OF THREE DIMENSIONAL LETTERS. THE LETTER FORMS HAVE AN OPEN, FLOWING CHARACTER THAT CAN BE USED IN THREE DIMENSIONAL APPLICATIONS.
55.	THREE DIMENSIONAL A & B IN VERTICAL APPLICATION
56.	THREE DIMENSIONAL A & B IN HORIZONTAL APPLICATION
57.	THREE DIMENSIONAL A & B IN COMBINED VERTICAL AND HORIZONTAL APPLICATION.
58.	ABCDE IN SINGLE STRIPE ALPHABET. AT THE PRESENT TIME, WE ARE DEVELOPING AN ALPHABET BASED ON THE SAME GEOMETRY AS THE LOGO, BUT USING ONLY A SINGLE STRIPE TO DEFINE EACH LETTER OR NUMBER.

DESIGN PROGRAM – PAGE FIVE

SLIDE #   COMMENT

59.   THIRTEEN WHITE STARS ON BLUE FIELD
        OUR NATION BEGAN WITH 13 COLONIES. THE STAR SYMBOL IS
        SAID TO REPRESENT THE HEAVENS AND THE DIVINE GOAL TO
        WHICH MAN HAS ASPIRED FROM TIME IMMEMORIAL

60.   50 STARS ON BLUE FIELD
        AT THIS TIME WE ARE 50 STATES – THE 50 STARS REPRESENT
        THE STATES COLLECTIVELY, NOT INDIVIDUALLY

61.   ARROW OF 50 STARS
        THE STARS IN THE HEAVENS MOVE, AND THIS MOVEMENT IS SAID
        TO TELL MANY THINGS. A SYSTEM OF SYMBOLS COULD BE DE-
        VELOPED BY MOVING THE 50 STARS.

62.   STAR TORCH
        BICENTENNIAL ACTIVITIES RELATED TO OUR EDUCATION PROGRAMS
        MIGHT USE THE TORCH SYMBOL

63.   STAR LONGHORN
        EACH STATE AND TERRITORY WILL HAVE ITS FOCAL WEEK. A
        SYMBOL USING THE 50 STARS COULD BE DEVELOPED FOR THIS
        USE.

64.   OLYMPIC SYMBOLS IN STARS
        10 STARS PER RING – 5 RINGS

65.   OLYMPIC SYMBOL IN STARS IN WHITE
        WINTER OLYMPICS

66.   STARBELL   –   EAGLE
&   THE STAR SYSTEM, BY COMBINING WITH WELL KNOWN NATIONAL
67.   MOTIFS, CAN BE USED TO SYMBOLIZE PROGRAMS WITH NATIONAL
        SCOPE: HERITAGE '76, HORIZONS '76, etc.

68.   STAR EAGLE AND '76 LOGO
        THE STAR SYSTEM WOULD BE INTEGRATED WITH THE LOGO

69.   LOGO WITH LINE RECTANGLE ABOVE
        OTHER PERTINANT INFORMATION CAN BE INTEGRATED WITH THE
        LOGO IN A SPACE ABOVE THE LOGO

70.   GERMAN AND ITALIAN COLORS INTEGRATED WITH LOGO.
        THE MANY TRANSLATORS NECESSARY TO SERVICE THE MANY FOREIGN
        VISITORS AT EVENTS CAN HAVE THEIR COUNTRY'S LANGUAGE
        SYMBOLIZED

71.   DIRECTIONAL SIGN GENERATING FROM LOGO.
        A DIRECTIONAL SYSTEM COULD BE DEVELOPED BY UTILIZING THE
        CAPABILITY OF THE LOGO TO EXPAND

DESIGN PROGRAM - PAGE SIX

SLIDE #	COMMENT
72.	WHEAT DEVELOPED FROM LOGO EXTENSION A COMPUTER SERVICE COULD BE CREATED THAT COULD FURNISH SANCTIONED ACTIVITIES WITH REPRODUCABLE ART WORK SPECIFICALLY DESIGNED FOR THE SPECIFIC EVENT. THIS WOULD BE A GREAT AID IN COORDINATING THE OVERALL PROGRAM BY AIDING THOSE AREAS WHERE PROFESSIONAL SERVICE WAS NOT AVAILABLE.
73.	HAPPY BIRTHDAY USA 200 YEARS OLD, 200 CANDLES
74.	THE LOGO
75.	THE LOGO INVERTED 2 **FOR** 200 YEARS

OUR ANTICIPATED MONTHLY REIMBURSABLE COSTS, BASED ON FOUR PEOPLE
WORKING 100 HOURS PER MONTH AT AN AVERAGE RATE OF $15.00 PER HOUR
IS $6,000 PER MONTH.

IN DECEMBER, I AM MOVING MY OFFICE FROM MEXICO CITY TO NEW YORK CITY.
OTHER REIMBURSABLE COSTS, SUCH AS TRAVEL EXPENSES, WOULD DEPEND ON
WHEN THE NINETY DAY PROJECT WOULD BEGIN.

IT IS UNDERSTOOD THAT I WOULD BE AVAILABLE FOR CONSULTATIONS SUB-
SEQUENT TO COMPLETION OF THE INITIAL DESIGN PROGRAM FOR NEW APPLI-
CATIONS AND REFINEMENTS. NORMALLY, MY FEE FOR THIS TYPE OF SERVICE
IS $30.00 PER HOUR.

Lance Wyman
LANCE WYMAN

Lance Wyman: Process.
A proposal for the 1976 USA Bicentennial identity.

Unit 41

Interview:	Adrian Shaughnessy
Editor:	Mark Sinclair
Design:	spin.co.uk
	Tony Brook, Claudia Klat
Design Assistant:	Tim Frei
Production Manager:	Edie Lippa
Publishing Director:	Patricia Finegan
Typeface:	Suisse International
Printer:	Göteborgs Tryckeriet
ISBN:	978-1-9164573-1-7

post@uniteditions.com

© 2018 Unit Editions

Unit Editions titles can be ordered direct from the publisher: uniteditions.com.

All rights reserved. No part of this publication may be reproduced or transmitted in any form or by any means, electronic or mechanical, including photocopy, recording or any informational storage and retrieval system, without prior permission from the publisher.

A catalogue for this book is available from the British Library.

Images: Every effort has been made to trace and contact the copyright holders of the images reproduced in this book. However, the publishers would be pleased, if informed, to correct any errors or omissions in subsequent editions of this publication.

Unit Editions would like to thank Lance Wyman for allowing us to publish this unique insight into his conceptual and working processes. We are grateful for his unfailing good humour and generosity. Thanks also to Neila Wyman for her support and friendship.

Embroidery by Neila Wyman

uniteditions.com